Brief Encounters
stories of love, sex & travel

Edited by
Michelle de Kretser

LONELY PLANET PUBLICATIONS
Melbourne • Oakland • London • Paris

Brief Encounters: stories of love, sex & travel

Published by Lonely Planet Publications
    Head Office: PO Box 617, Hawthorn, Vic 3122, Australia
    Branches: 155 Filbert St, Suite 251, Oakland, CA 94607, USA
                        10a Spring Place, London NW5 3BH, UK
                        71 bis rue du Cardinal Lemoine, 75005 Paris, France

Published 1998

Printed by SNP Printing Pte Ltd, Singapore

Designed by Margaret Jung
Copy-edited by Janet Austin
Photographs of roses by Olivier Cirendini

National Library of Australia Cataloguing in Publication Data

Brief encounters : stories of love, sex & travel

ISBN 0 86442 529 5.

1. Travel – Fiction. 2. Erotic stories. 3. Love stories.
I. de Kretser, Michelle.

A823.301

Introduction, selection and biographical notes © Lonely Planet 1998
Additional copyright information appears on pp. 285–7

Contents

Introduction

Michelle de Kretser is the publisher of Lonely Planet's travel literature series, Journeys.

Thinking about it

Weren't we all familiar with the scenario? I asked, presenting the idea to Lonely Planet. Hadn't we all fantasised about meeting that perfect stranger on the road? And didn't we agree that falling in love with a person was the surest way of falling in love with a place? A sigh of recognition – *Oooh, yes* – wafted around that roomful of inveterate travellers.

Just why are new people and different places so alluring, I wondered. Perhaps because strangers provide us with the opportunity of becoming strangers to ourselves: 'you make me feel brand new' is a sentiment echoed by lovers and travellers alike and it carries an addictive charge not to be underestimated.

The book I had in mind would invite exploration of the imaginative links which turned travel and romance into metaphors for each other: the seductive promises of change and renewal, the appeal of seeing and being seen afresh. It would encourage reflection on the treacherous potential for disillusionment inherent in the late twentieth century's terminal fascination with the new and the exotic.

'Make sure they're true stories,' urged a colleague, 'readers want to know what really happened, what it was really like.' But where does autobiography shade into fiction, experience into imagination? Readers and writers have the advantage over travellers of being able to come and go freely over frontiers, so why not disregard those arbitrary delineations? This book would bring together fiction, nonfiction and stories that serenely inhabited the shadowlands between.

It would also include original work alongside previously published material, offering responses which consciously addressed a theme as well as an overview of how writers had dealt with the subject when caught off-guard: posed photos jumbled in among candid-camera shots. I suggested to various writers whose work I admired, and who took a literary interest in travel, that they consider writing about romantic encounters involving people who were away from home. Romantic encounters, I was keen to specify, in the broadest sense: passionate flings, affairs which happened only in the head, erotic one-nighters, disastrous pick-ups . . . Or even – just possibly – romantic in the narrowest sense of happy-ever-after.

In other words, I was grudgingly prepared to concede the possibility of happy endings. But mostly I was anticipating endings, since the great thing about travel, as Lawrence Millman once said, is that it allows you to unmeet people. The essence of travel, I thought, the definition of desire: brief encounters.

Doing it

That unprecedentedly searing Melbourne summer, I searched for stories of love and sex and travel. I read romance anthologies and travel writing, short stories and essays, literary and not-so-literary magazines.

In air-conditioned public libraries I found myself reading collection after collection of erotica under the cool gaze of public librarians.

I read books borrowed from friends, books sent from the States and the UK by colleagues, books recommended in other books. There were dead-end books which wound up nowhere, books which encouraged lingering, books which invited exploration and opened up unexpected vistas.

Unsurprisingly, I discovered that writers of erotica rarely concerned themselves with questions of travel or place; I should have known that in erotic literature what you're doing is far more significant than where you're doing it. Less predictably, I also discovered that many travel writers didn't go in for romantic encounters. Or if they did, they weren't telling: whether from prudence or prudishness, good manners or bad conscience, was a matter of conjecture.

Women travel writers were more recklessly confessional than their male counterparts. I wondered if women whose work regularly took them away from home were less likely to be in committed relationships than men, with the result that they could be more open about their travel romances. Or was it that travel writing, searching for new directions, had shifted towards a confessional mode over the last decade, a period which co-incided with the increasing entry of women into the genre?

I noticed that the received image of a country or a landscape coloured the romances enacted there: Corsica was wild, hence suited to dramatic gestures and precipitate acts; the sensual Caribbean promoted languid love. China and Japan lent themselves to nuanced half-tones – a sigh, a wistful falling away; Italy was spontaneity with operatic undertows of crime and passion. Several writers explicitly explored the connection between the expectations people had of a place and what happened to them when they got there; travel, like falling in love, was thus bound up with mythology, with telling and being told stories.

As file cards and Post-its proliferated around me, I wanted only to keep going: 'Dear Lonely Planet, Having fun. Please send more money.' Stories beckoned like far horizons but deadlines were looming overhead: it was time to call a halt to exploration and settle down to the business of putting a book together.

When I re-read the stories I'd picked out over the summer I found that in some cases – as with other kinds of indiscretion – I couldn't exactly recall what the attraction had ever been; a little shamefacedly, I hit my Delete key – gone, gone, goodbye. Other decisions were harder to make. Being both the editor and publisher of *Brief Encounters* definitely had its advantages, but there were occasions when it was impossible for me to reconcile the editorial desire to be partisan with the publishing imperative to be dispassionate; I was rescued from that impasse by other readers, whose detached response to the stories helped whittle down the list.

Finally, a certain amount of natural selection took place: some writers wanted higher fees than the editorial budget could afford, others missed their production deadlines, a few steadfastly ignored all requests for permission to publish their work. (Just as I was about to give it up as a lost cause, I received permission to include a story I had chased for months with increasing urgency by letter, fax and phone.) Time and money are seldom mentioned in introductions to anthologies but they are present in every set of editorial choices nevertheless.

For judicious assistance with arranging the stories I turned to Janet Austin, the editor with whom I worked at Lonely Planet. Stories about beginnings at the start of the anthology, we agreed, and stories about endings at the end. And in between? Crouched over photocopies spread out on the floor, Janet and I shuffled and ordered and re-ordered the selection. I wanted stories to jostle each other stylistically; Janet pointed out the need for variation in length and location.

At home that night, I picked up an anthology I had bought some weeks previously and started reading. I began with a story in the middle of the book because I recognised the author's name, read on in order automatically for a few pages, skipped back to the start because an intriguing title caught my eye, got a bit bored and flipped to the end . . . Editors are obliged to map out itineraries, but readers possess an inspired facility for wandering off track.

Ending it

I read them through one last time, the twenty stories that made up *Brief Encounters*. And realised, with a small jolt, that they surprised me in one significant respect: I had envisaged an anthology which would valorise restlessness over coming to rest, but here were stories shot through with a longing for landfall. Brief encounters, perhaps – but if only the world had been otherwise, if only we could have stayed.

In the end, compiling *Brief Encounters* was an affair of anticipation and improvisation, of serendipitous choices and inevitable regrets, of desire indulged and expectations overturned.

Like love, like travel.

My thanks to: Jennifer Cox, who came up with the title; Leonie Mugavin, who tirelessly tracked down books for me; Jim Hart, Tony Wheeler, Maureen Wheeler, Carolyn Miller, Jen Morris and Carly Hammond, who commented on the selection; Christina Thompson and Paul Smitz for good advice about the introduction; and Janet Austin, who copy-edited Brief Encounters, *compiled the contributors' notes and was an indispensable companion on the journey.*

Prelude

from
An Indian Attachment

Sarah Lloyd

Sarah Lloyd was born in London in 1947. She is an inveterate traveller, and the author of *An Indian Attachment* and *Chinese Characters*.

F or three days I had been in an Indian train, crossing the country from its western extremity in Gujerat to Calcutta in the east. The company had been as unexciting as the landscape; I'd been stuck in a carriage full of tedious people all grumbling about how tedious everyone else was. One little girl had found me so tedious (sitting reading a history of the Sikhs all the way) that she'd given me a sharp slap to wake me up. I gave her one back and her father laughed, whereupon we all fell back into collective boredom until the lush watery landscape of Bengal announced the proximity of Calcutta.

It was wonderful to be out of the train and back in the familiar chaos and electric energy of the bazaar street life. It was nice to be welcomed by big smiles from people who knew me at the gurdwara. And in the corner of the sleeping hall a man was sitting cross-legged on a blanket, with the long black beard of the tenth Sikh Guru, and the eyes of Buddha, sweeping up at the corners.

He had a powerful face that instantly compelled me: high forehead, long nose and skin the colour of almonds; but the eyes suggested sadness, a past full of grief. On his head he wore a dome of blue turbans. A length of orange fabric was tied around the waist of his aquamarine tunic, and a second piece hung over his shoulder, loose. In front of him lay a sword.

Jungli was a Nihang, a self-elected member of an informal religious army maintained by the Sikhs for the defence of their faith. The clothes he wore, the code he followed and the ideals he lived by had survived unaltered the 300 years of their existence.

At that time I was going through a being-charitable-to-

Nihangs phase. Many were poor and some were homeless; as far as I could tell they were dependent on the generosity of others. I had been told they were prepared to forfeit their lives in defending their faith, yet few ordinary Sikhs showed them either kindness or respect. Returning from the bazaar later on in the evening I bought Jungli milk sweets and fruit.

*

Gurdwaras are open to people of all faiths. For more than four centuries they have offered hospitality free of charge, providing basic sleeping and washing facilities and two simple meals a day. Arriving on the night mail from Assam two months previously, this Calcutta gurdwara had been the first I ever stayed in. I had set off across Howrah Bridge and into the bazaar streets, and every now and then I asked someone, "Where's the gurdwara?"

Blank look. No English.

"Where's the gurdwara?"

"Excuse me. I am not understanding your English."

"But it's an Indian word! Gurdwara. Sikh temple."

"Oh you mean gurdwara! No gurdwara is here."

Then again, "Where's the gurdwara?"

"You go straight. Then ask."

"Where's the gurdwara?"

"It's my idea there's one near Victoria Memorial, next to hospital."

But other people seemed to think there was one in the bazaar somewhere. I spotted a Sikh taxi driver. He was bound to know.

"Where's the gurdwara?"

Shrug. Not religious. Not interested.

Gradually I tracked it down and the answers became more

optimistic: "Straight on. This side." But I still missed it, for the street frontage was just a plain white doorway in the crowded bazaar, among shops, stalls and pavement hawkers; deceivingly, for it was in fact a large eight-storey building. I learnt to recognise the doorway afterwards by means of a colossal Gwalior Suiting advertisement on the opposite side of the road. Those Gwalior Suiting signs were all over India, I discovered later; everywhere, that was, except Gwalior, where the rage was something else.

Inside the doorway stood a man in a blue turban holding a long spear. "Gurdwara?" I asked, and he pointed to a staircase. On the first floor was a big stark room that I took to be the place of worship, and above it was a gallery. On the third floor I found an office, locked. I sat down and waited.

"Have you any rooms?" I asked when a lean man, also in a blue turban, materialised.

No English, but from what I could gather no rooms either.

I sat down again. I had spent all morning looking for this gurdwara. But then a little girl appeared and beckoned to me, and I followed her up three more flights of stairs, past a school and an eating hall, on to the sixth floor.

It was just what I had hoped for, a large communal hall with windows all round and people's washing hanging on strings in front of them. The floor was covered in Panjabi daris. And that was all. Everyone chose a pitch and parked himself in it, his luggage against the wall. There were men sprawled across the daris chatting in groups, while others snored on their bedding or tied their turbans. In the corner was what seemed to be a semi-permanent camp of a young Bengali mother and her children; they were cooking lunch.

As evening fell more and more people turned up. They were

15

still turning up at ten and eleven at night. Most of them were businessmen with attaché cases (which they used as pillows) coming to the city to buy parts or meet a client. They lay down as they were, fully dressed, having cleared the dust from the patch of dari they fancied by swatting it with their towel. The turban acted as padding against the hard edges of their cases; they placed their shoes neatly beside their feet.

The lights stayed on all night, full on, and at two or three in the morning the first contingent, the most devout, began to get up. They shuffled across the hall to the washing cubicles in the corner (from which loud splashing and singing and gurgling noises were originating) and returned chattering their teeth to start morning prayer. Their mumbling and chanting was punctuated by the snores and wind of the businessmen and accompanied by the next shift in the bathroom. What I had to learn was that Indians could sleep at any hour of day or night and that darkness had no particular significance for them.

Calcutta was, and still is, my favourite Indian city. Every day I wandered along the banks of the river and watched the sun set over Howrah Station. Every day I returned to the gurdwara along the same dark back streets, where every other doorway revealed a small Hindu shrine fairy-lit by strings of naked bulbs, the deity all but submerged beneath garlands of marigolds and the blue haze of incense. Every day I carried back sweetmeats for Jungli and his friends, Inderjit and Bir.

It was January and cold. Jungli got up at four every morning, took his bath and came back shivering, sat wrapped in his blanket and recited prayers till six. I, meanwhile, would be reading

Tagore, or standing on the roof eight storeys above the Mahatma Gandhi Road watching herds of goats clattering down its dark ravine past the sheeted street sleepers towards the Ganges. After tea at six we helped prepare the food for the morning meal, sitting in a circle on the daris, peeling onions, shelling ginger and cutting up potatoes, conversing in signs and nursery school Hindi and laughing at our misunderstandings.

Jungli, Inderjit and Bir had travelled 1500 miles to Calcutta from Amritsar in Panjab, on the tail of Bir's runaway brother; he had escaped with money belonging to his joint family, and was making for the fast life in Bangkok. Several times each day they went to his hotel by Howrah Station and tried to persuade him to return to his home and Inderjit's sister, his wife. But Bir's brother had other ideas.

One morning while we were peeling the vegetables, I noticed Inderjit take something from his pocket, pull off small pieces and hand them round. He gave a lump to me and I swallowed it like everyone else, wondering what it could be but determined to find out. Getting off a tram in Chowringee an hour later my head began to reel, so I entered a mosque and lay down on the floor.

"A white woman, an infidel, lying on the floor of the holy mosque! Get up! Get out!"

An infidel intoxicated by opium, no less.

Back in the gurdwara, the ceiling doing strange things above my head, Jungli fed me with pieces of orange.

Our unspoken attachment deepened. I was moved by his tenderness, his simplicity and his beautiful eyes. Beauty is a great robber of my common sense. I tried not to be affected by it; tried to avoid him. I knew it to be outside the bounds of the religion he followed. And I was a traveller.

Another thing was that hair.

Having fought all my life against my own hair being cut, I was sympathetic towards the no-cutting tradition of the Sikhs. And I agreed with them when, in answer to the provocative Hindu/Muslim, "Why don't you cut your hair?" they replied, "The question is not why don't we cut our hair, but why do you cut yours?" It was partly because of their long hair that Hindus and Muslims found Sikhs objectionable: the fact that they had to look different. They resented their proud bearing (only they referred to it as arrogance); they disliked their straightforwardness, their determination and their refusal to be put down. That, to them, was aggression.

The Sikhs' hair didn't like being imprisoned in a turban all its life, let out only for washing and daily grooming. Most men didn't have that much of it, but occasionally I had seen a man with really long thick hair. I had come across one several weeks previously, in a crowd of Hindus on the steps of the bathing ghats in Benares. Pilgrims were swarming over the ghats, dunking themselves in the holy Ganges, thumping wet saris on the stones and bounding after runaway children. In their midst sat a Sikh, alone and serene, slowly and deliberately combing an avalanche of black hair. The Hindus wore white and red and pink and green but the Sikh wore black: black trousers, black shirt. He was a Daramaraj, a god of Death, among the gaily chattering living. I was transfixed. I could no more avert my eyes than the enchanted sailors could cease gazing at the mermaid on the rock.

He finished combing his hair and melted, an unreal shadow, into the multitude. I wondered how I was ever going to live without him.

Now again, the same thing.

Every morning after the communal tea, Jungli placed a small mirror on the blanket in front of him and combed his hair. It took

him half an hour. I watched surreptitiously as he unwound the
five lengths of turban material obligatory to a Nihang, fearing
that I was trespassing on some secret and intimate act. He leant
forward and loosened his hair, which fell in a torrent to the floor.
There was red in its black where it strayed loose as he combed
it, and blue in its sheen when it lay in a mass and caught the light.
I pretended to read a book. He rubbed it with coconut oil, combed
it again in long slow strokes from the back of his neck, twisted
it into a rope and tied it in a double knot on top of his head. He
took each piece of turban material, stretched it taut along a
diagonal axis and rolled the fabric towards the centre. Then,
securing the front end between his teeth and jerking his head like
a bird so he could see the relevant part in the mirror, he wound
it round his head, smoothly and symmetrically, coiling the free
end like a slack python after each revolution.

On my fifth day in Calcutta, Jungli, Inderjit and Bir took me
sightseeing. We took the tram through Calcutta to Kalighat and
walked through narrow dirty lanes to Kali Mandir, a big Hindu
temple devoted to the goddess Kali, where I noticed a lot of goats
and blood on the floor and wanted to get out. But the others were
looking on with interest. When I heard the chop of an axe and
the thud of a goat's head hitting the ground, I left without them.

"Why do Hindus sanctify one animal and cut off the head of
another?" I tried to ask them when they caught up with me, but
my Hindi wasn't up to it and they didn't understand. I spoke no
Panjabi and Jungli not a word of English.

"Never mind," was the gist of what they said when they saw
that for some reason I hadn't appreciated the goats. "We'll go
and see something else."

We went on down the road and up the drive of a very ugly
modern building. It looked like a crematorium. "What's this?" I

asked. I understood two words of the answer: "Electric programme." It *was* a crematorium.

Hindus and Sikhs burned their dead on big open bonfires: crematoria were a recent innovation in India and not wholly approved of, appearing in the cities as a result of the scarcity of firewood. We were lucky, they said, there was a death ceremony in progress. A decrepit corpse scantily covered with a sheet was being washed with ghee and sprinkled with sandalwood by the tearful next-of-kin, whose suffering was much worse than the sight of the body. Jungli and Bir had seen crematoria before and remained in the background, but Inderjit and I stood in the front row among the relatives and watched with a morbid fascination.

At the end of a week it was time to leave; I had already stayed too long. Jungli, Inderjit and Bir were returning, defeated, to Amritsar, and I was catching a train to Bangladesh. We went down into the street and headed for the hotel to make a final assault on Bir's recalcitrant brother. Inderjit and Bir walked ahead. In the middle of the crowded Howrah Bridge, trams squealing, structure creaking, cartmasters cursing, rickshaw wallahs shouting, engines stalling, beggars wailing, horns hooting, wheels rattling, feet thundering, Jungli said, "I love you."

I looked at him. I didn't know he knew any English. The words sounded unreal. Then he was swallowed up in the crowd.

He came with me next morning to Sealdah Station.

"When are you coming to Amritsar?" he asked again and again as we waited for my train. He had plenty of time in which to do so as we were on the wrong platform.

"In about a month," I hazarded. I don't follow an itinerary when I'm travelling, and I find that sort of question hard to answer. I told him to love God and forget about me, for just as I was leaving Calcutta I would also leave Amritsar. God, on the other hand, wasn't going anywhere.

When my train eventually left, we didn't even touch hands. I watched him standing on the disappearing platform, a lone figure in blue holding a sword, diminished by the great Victorian canopy of Sealdah Station. Two hours later I was in Bangladesh.

Hot Tin Roof

from
Summers with Juliet

Bill Roorbach

Bill Roorbach is a writer and lecturer who has taught at the University of Maine, the University of Vermont and the Ohio State University. His work, both fiction and nonfiction, has appeared in many magazines and journals, including the *New York Times* magazine, *Harper's*, *Poets and Writers*, the *Philadelphia Inquirer* and *Newsday*.

At eight I was interested in fishing, reading and the diligent scavenging of fabulous pieces of glass and metal and, sometimes, wood. I have clear memories of specific finds: a blue glass insulator from a fallen telephone pole; a railroad spike from the tracks behind Mike Didelot's; hundreds of thin, unidentified strips of metal that I found on the streets of my lonely new home town. I found coins and bike pedals and spoons and, once, an old cast-iron witch's pot. I even had a weathered board with Chinese writing on it, which I'd found floated up at the beach on Long Island Sound. How far had it come? (Well, probably from Stamford or Norwalk or New York, but I had a grander vision.)

At eight I knew about an old truck in the woods way back behind our house, a Model A I thought, the lord of all treasures, with speedometer and steering wheel intact. I also knew about an old steamer trunk which sat half-buried in leaves just off Jelliff Mill Road. I had spied it from the height of the school bus, kept it secret from all but Mike Didelot, convinced it was full of jewels or some poor prince's head or a giant gladiator's outsized armour. When Mike and I finally broke into the trunk, the flowerpots were treasure enough, three of them, at least a little bit ancient, and broken.

And when I was eight, unbeknownst to me, Juliet Karelsen was born, 15 June 1962, away off in New York City, that tall town where my father worked and where a penny could kill. By the time Juliet herself had turned eight she was already an independent little New York girl, owner of an elaborate doll's house, maker of 200 faces, eater of ice cream, seller on the street of homemade greeting cards, rogue child of Central Park West, in charge of her parents, in love with her teacher, in cahoots with the doormen, going steady with a black boy from school, studying ethics, playing guitar, husbanding a hamster named Willy. So sensitive, said a family friend, that she could feel the grass grow under her feet. That summer, Juliet, bearing her hamster, and in league with her little sister Eva, deigned to accompany her parents to Wellfleet, Massachusetts, on Cape Cod. I was sixteen by then, about to turn seventeen, and Juliet and I had kept our relative distance. New York City, New York, to New Canaan, Connecticut, is about forty-five miles. Wellfleet, Cape Cod, to Edgartown, Martha's Vineyard, is also about forty-five miles, and in Edgartown I was on vacation with my own family.

I had to go to bird sanctuaries and museums and clothes stores and nature walks and church. We went to the beach in the mornings for a prescribed number of hours, then came home to the hotel for lunch. I baby-sat Janet while picking on Dougie and Carol, then in the afternoon was set free for three or four hours. I knew just where to go. In Edgartown you hung out on the lawn in front of the Old Whaling Church with cool kids from all over, kids who knew what it was all about. And on the Vineyard, when it wasn't all about how long your bleached hair was getting, it was all about James Taylor. There was always a party being rumoured and J.T. was always going to be at the party.

On the Cape, Juliet meanwhile would have been building a beach house for her doll family, a group made up of little European dolls. Hans and Bridget: the parents; Susie, Debbie, Peter, David, Frank, Louisa and Christopher: the children; and Uncle Nick: their live-in dentist. Juliet and Eva and their friends sawed boards in the basement of her family's rented cottage until the doll's house was done. There was no workbench in the basement, and no vices, just a saw and hammer and a pile of lumber; so Juliet made the other three hold on to the old boards, six skinny arms taut and trembling, as she sawed and hammered, intent on the work. When the other girls wanted to stop, Juliet said no. The doll family must have a beach house!

*

My seventeenth birthday came in the midst of vacation. As a treat I got to go out on my own; was given a midnight curfew. A wild luxury. Especially since I knew of a party at which not only James Taylor was guaranteed to show, but his brother Livingston too, and probably Carole King. The party of the summer. I dressed in my tightest black blue-jeans and my hippest BVD undershirt (that brand had a *pocket*) and flipped my hair many times in front of the wavy hotel mirror.

The party was at an elegant old house, clapboard, square, white, the home once of a whaling captain, and now, having not changed hands all these 200 years, summer home of his progeny. Its door was painted red and was open. The music of Jimi Hendrix blared forth.

I gulped; gave my head a shake; marched up the steps of the austere porch. No one asked who I was. I accepted a mug full of wine, lit up a cigarette and found my way into the living room and then to the hearth, where I could lean under the great mantelpiece and watch the proceedings. James Taylor did not yet seem to be in attendance. Indeed, no one older than eighteen seemed to be in attendance. I drank more wine; smoked another cigarette. I had a beer someone passed me; smoked a little pot. More wine. A drink of Jack Daniels. Some beer. Some wine. I never moved from my spot. On the mantel was an array of

27

objects, all of which held real interest for me. An antique sextant. A large marine vertebra. An old, well-used bos'n's pipe. A real harpoon. A walrus tusk, scrimshawed. A baleen comb, made from the great plankton-screening maw of a sperm whale. Gradually I got drunk enough to forget the party and to pay attention to the treasures. A shark's jaw with triple rows of teeth. When had this shark swum? A little stone Buddha. How far had Captain Pendergast (that was the name engraved on a brass box) sailed? A pair of brass-and-leather binoculars. A glass float, round as the Earth and as blue, escaped from a fisherman's net in Portugal, I knew, but when? And around the room, photographs and paintings and etchings: grinning second mates, sheets of blubber, boats under full sail and adorned with flags and fresh paint and men in the rigging, leaving Edgartown harbour.

The Pendergasts also had a clock collection, thirty or forty old things, well kept and tocking. They all struck at midnight, a prolonged concatenation of bongs and dings and whistles and tweets. I stayed. Silly curfew! The party was going strong, doors closed, windows closed, music very low in fear of the ever-watchful Edgartown police. James Taylor on the stereo, as close as we would get to him that night. Someone had handed me a full jug of wine and I clutched it, staring up at a trio of rudely carved, life-sized, wooden geese. Full of wine, I spoke my first words of the night: "I wonder what those geese were for?"

Soon a knot of us were sharing the wine and discussing the dustless birds. Too unmarked to have been used by any hunter as decoys. "Too top heavy, anyway," someone said, poking at one. "Not weighted at all." Each goose had a reddish glass eye, and feet painted onto its bottom. We argued. A young woman came up, the young woman who was throwing the party, a good forty or sixty pounds overweight, somewhat older than I, eyes brown and slightly occluded by her chubby cheeks as she smiled. "They're boredom geese," she said. "My great-great-great-grandfather made 'em whenever he got stuck on land for too long."

The clocks, all thirty or forty of them, struck one. Ms Pendergast, our hostess (her first name, I think, was Roberta), showed me a box of scrimshaw tools. And two narwhal tusks, the likes of which were once sold as unicorn horns. And a coconut-shell mask from Tahiti, made at the time Gauguin lived there. And a block of wood with leather straps, once some ancestor's replacement foot. The log of the frigate *Margaret*, dated 1807, which my hostess wasn't supposed to open, but did. Upstairs, Roberta showed me her bed, which had been the captain's bed on the good ship *Eleanor Alison*, circa 1830. Quickly, she got me out of her room as if her mother were about to catch us, and down the back stairs. In the kitchen were thirty more carved geese, a flight of them on two long shelves that met in the corner over the stove. "A vee," as she pointed out. "Like a real flock."

Downstairs, the party had dissipated to a few drunks and my tour guide's younger brothers. The latter were busy bouncing the former. The house was a mess. Soon, I noticed, everyone was gone but the two brothers, Ms Pendergast and I. My head was beginning to spin, the prelude to a night of vomiting in the shower while my father, disgusted, held me upright in the stall. "Mom's going to kill us," the youngest brother said.

"Who is this guy?" the other said, pointing at me with a back-flung thumb.

Spinning or not I lifted the big green jug of wine to my lips.

"My friend," Roberta said. She certainly was fat, a good deal bigger than I.

"Well, Mom's going to kill us," brother number one repeated, with special emphasis. The brothers were not fat, not at all.

I pressed on, undaunted. "What's that thing?" I said, pointing.

"Blubber knife," the bigger brother said, annoyed. "Time to go."

Ms Pendergast and her brothers walked me out on the porch. She shooed the boys inside and, apparently having mistaken my interest in her family artefacts for an interest in herself, she took my head in her hands and kissed me smack smack on the lips. Her hands on my head seemed to contain the spinning somewhat and her lips gave the whole fuzzy world a warm, wet focus. I put my arms around some of her, for support, and there we stood, lip to lip, till her brother came out and pulled her inside.

On the Cape, Juliet and her family must have been asleep after a night engaged in one of their ritual vacation activities. The Drive-in, Provincetown, the Dairy King, the Puritan Shop in Wellfleet. (On a recent camping trip she showed me everything: their various rented houses; the houses of her friends, Meyer, Winkelstein, DeCarlo, Waters; the Howard Johnson's her family always stopped at; the beaches they had most fun at; the place she bought her best bathing suit *ever*.) Juliet and Eva preferred the Buzzard's Bay side of the Cape where low tide made miles of flats to play on and everyone bragged of knowing someone who had walked to Provincetown across the sandbars before high tide came to drown him. The girls played marina, using shells as boats and digging channels which the tide would fill, rising. They stole *Once is Never Enough* from their mother and read the sex scenes to each other as they lay under their towels in the sand. They brought Willy the hamster to the dunes so he could see the ocean and to Howard Johnson's so he wouldn't be lonely at home or too hot in the car.

My father at midnight was miffed. At one o'clock he was furious and worried, each emotion escalating the other. At two o'clock he went out looking for me. He got in the car (a wood-panelled station wagon) and crawled the streets of Edgartown with his lights off. Earlier he and Mom had taken note of a party at one of the old captain's houses, so he slunk over to that neighbourhood and found me, sure enough, on the porch in the near dark kissing someone as big around as he was.

I went to Martha's Vineyard next in 1980 at the behest of my old college friend Jon Zeeman. I could afford the trip because I'd spotted a classified ad in the *New York Times* looking for someone to write a question-and-answer format home-repair book. (I got to New York four hours early for my appointment, stumbled through the interview, actually *fell* on my way out of the publisher's office, but got the job. Ten dollars a page for a 256-page book, 2560 dollars, not much for a whole book, even at the time, but to me a fortune.) I told my then girlfriend Melanie I thought I'd try writing it on the Vineyard. Maybe by myself. She cried. I cried. Everybody cried, but I was determined to go and she was determined to let me.

When Jon came, I was ready. He had rented a U-Haul for his PA system and his amps and his Hammond organ. He meant to have a band and play for the summer tourists. We emptied my little house of everything I owned, which wasn't much, mostly odd bits of pipe and lumber and boxes of books, and headed for the Vineyard, Jon with his guitars up front in the car, me with my typewriter and my tools. In Oak Bluffs, fresh off the ferry, we took possession of 222 Circuit Avenue, a rickety old gingerbread cottage with six bedrooms, which would make room for the other two-thirds of Jon's jazz trio when they turned up and for two or three oddball room-mates to help pay the rent.

On sunny days our little household went to the beach. On the rare rainy days, Jon and his band rehearsed upstairs, thumping the floor. I typed in the basement, one or two frantic days a week, making the book. *Fix-It! Tips and Tricks for Home Repair*. Every fifty pages I'd send off to New York, then haunt the general delivery window at the post office until my cheque (500 dollars!) would arrive. I tried to make the questions sound like real people talking; used a lot of exclamation marks to show their excitement at the task ahead. *Q: My darn faucet is driving me crazy! How can I get it to stop dripping all night?* or *Q: I'd like to build a bookshelf to keep this home repair book in. How do I go about it?* or *Q: My son Johnny* [I always used my friend's names] *just had a snowball fight to end all snowball fights! How do you repair a broken window?*

At night, Jon's trio, the Circuit Avenue Band, played around the island, at bars, at restaurants, at parties. I went along and the four of us managed to meet a lot of women, which, after all, was the idea.

Juliet, being only eighteen, may or may not have been too young for our notice, though she was on Martha's Vineyard for a week that summer, visiting a college friend who was working as an up-island au pair. Jules was a freshman by then at the University of Michigan, had spent most of the summer working as a counsellor at a camp for disturbed kids, had had her own heart broken and learned what all those lyrics to all those James Taylor songs she liked to play on her guitar were really about.

The next summer, after an insolvent off-season in New York, Jon and the boys and I were back. Two summers later, we were back again. Jon and I found a cheap enough house near the sewage treatment plant on the outskirts of Edgartown, which only smelled when the wind came our way one night out of a week, or two. By now I was singing in Jon's summer band, which had evolved into a jazz/rock/oldies/rhythm-and-blues/country band, somehow, and being paid half what the other musicians were paid. We hadn't enough money for restaurant meals, much less enough for a decent beach towel or enough to fix our old bomb cars when they broke, but we had plenty of money for drinks at the bars, and plenty of money for admission to the Hot Tin Roof, which had been Carly Simon's place, a seventies-style disco in an old airplane hangar up in the scrub oak forest by the airport.

On the evening of 20 July I looked up from the bar there and spied a pretty young woman passing. She was blonde and flushed and had an aquiline nose (which word until recently I thought meant *straight*, but no, it means *like an eagle's*, hooked), and fairly glowed with aplomb. I kept my eye on her as she glided her way across the dance floor and up the stairs through the crowd to the bar.

Jon came waltzing by, holding a beer. "Have a look," I said.

He peered brazenly back up into the balcony area, found the table in question. "Blonde?" he asked.

I pretended not to look. "Right."

"Nothing special." And off he went.

I danced with friends nearer my age then – Sally from the Rare Duck, Messina from the beach, Ellie Winters from the bookstore – hoping to give the impression of my own popularity and insouciance. I drank beer. I danced. I went to the bathroom. When I came out, the blonde girl – Juliet – stood exactly in my way, having bypassed the line for the lady's room.

"Anyone in there?" she asked.

"I'll check."

She followed me in, scooted into a stall. "Could you watch the door?"

I deliberated. Then, not wanting to seem too easy, I abandoned my post.

Later, when I found her near the dance floor with her friends, she pretended not to know me.

"The men's room?" I said, to sharpen her memory.

"You!" she said. "There was a crowd of pissing guys in there when I came out!" It seemed she found this funny. She accepted my invitation to dance. She told me she lived with her sister and a couple of friends in Vineyard Haven. She told me she was from New York. She told me she worked in a sandwich place, dipping ice cream. She told me she played guitar.

I told her my name, which on the Vineyard was Billy.

"Oh!" she said, with real feeling. "I had a hamster once named Willy!"

*

Autumn comes early to the Vineyard. Leases expire on Labor Day. Flocks of geese start assembling for the flight south.

Juliet and I had formed a tenuous union which was about to be sundered by her trip back to Michigan. She seemed not the least troubled by that dark prospect. Late on one of our last nights, she decided we should sleep on the beach, away from the crowd of superannuated teenagers in my house and away from her basement apartment, where she and her three room-mates shared two small bedrooms equipped with but a double bed each.

Beach sleeping is not allowed on Martha's Vineyard. But we

surreptitiously borrowed Joanna's car and headed to South Beach, where I was sure we'd be caught and arrested. Jules knew a place, a dirt road that ended high over a salt pond, near a darkened house. We took along all the blankets from her bed and one pillow and several beers, and tramped like sleepwalking children across the dunes and to the beach. We walked up-island a long way, past another couple who were already asleep. Finally we stopped, spread out our blankets and felt the cold wind and watched the surf coming in under the brilliant Milky Way, Venus coruscating near Mars at the horizon; enough light despite the new moon to illuminate the spray and the crests of the marching waves and to silhouette flock after flock of night geese arriving at the pond behind us. We shivered in our blankets, sipping beer, talking softly, kissing.

After a brief hour we saw flashlights coming. We held our breath, watching the couple down the beach get arrested and waiting, Juliet calmly, I pumping adrenaline. But the flashlight beams could not reach us and the cops turned back, satisfied with their catch. By five in the morning we had slept very little, had made sandy love and had decided to head back, to be warm in the car as the dawn arrived in pink and mist.

The pond, when we got there, was covered, acre after acre, with geese. There were thousands and new flocks arriving moment by moment: a busy airport. Juliet and I watched them from the windless warmth of the car for an hour. At sunrise the flocks began to depart, out over the ocean, big flocks then lesser ones, away in a chorus of honks from their fellows. I have never seen so many geese in one place; in fact, I have never seen so many of any single animal gathered in one place, except humans, perhaps, and bees. I thought of Captain Pendergast's geese, unliving on their shelves.

I'd always thought of geese as the end of things, flying off in melancholy V's. I grew sad sitting there on the big bench seat of Joanna's old car, overlooking the salt pond, which had become the very heart of endings, sitting away from tousled Juliet, my friend. Hard to separate endings from beginnings at times like that. Hard to think, oh, *time will tell*, as bright new Juliet waves from the ferry two days later. Gone. Hard to keep the melancholy out of the letters I wrote her nearly daily, some on birch bark from New Hampshire (anything to impress), some on my brand-new letterhead from New York (anything, anything). Hard to recognise the beginning of something, but there it was. And all those silly geese departing.

New Cythera Again

Christina Thompson

Christina Thompson is the editor of the Australian literary magazine *Meanjin*. She grew up in Boston, has a PhD from the University of Melbourne and is married with two sons.

F or most people, travel is a matter of incident and gossip, of things that happen to you en route – the smell of diesel, a sidelong glance, a coconut falling on your roof – and things you read describing what happened to other people in the places where you are. These two sources, the encounters and the stories, tend to be mutually reinforcing, sometimes in peculiar ways.

Take the first time I visited Tahiti. I had very little money and everything was horribly expensive, with the consequence that I found it difficult to get enough to eat. After several lean days I finally discovered that the Chinese in Papeete are the best (and possibly the only) purveyors of cheap, hot meals, which they sell from trucks parked where working people congregate. I vividly remember the day I stumbled upon one of these food trucks for the first time, and how with every bite of meat and vegetables and steaming rice my flagging spirits rose.

At the time I was reading the missionary John Williams' account of his visit to the island of Mangaia in 1830. Not surprisingly, the passage that caught my eye had to do with food. As the fishing off Mangaia was poor and rats the only animals on the island, these were consumed by the locals with great relish. 'Indeed,' wrote Williams, 'a common expression with them when speaking of anything delicious was "It is as sweet as a rat".' Despite our unchanged habit of looking upon rats as 'exceedingly disgusting', I was so hungry that even a rat in the right circumstances might have looked like food. Indeed, I occasionally wondered if it wasn't rat I was eating.

On this, my first trip to the Pacific, I carried a 1949 anthology called *The Spell of the Pacific*. It had a suitably lurid dustjacket showing the mauve mountains of a high island, its green coastal plain and, in the foreground, a cluster of lateen-rigged canoes sailing on a coral sea, all framed by a bit of beach grass and a fringe of black palm. It was full of accounts of explorers and travellers, a few novelists and poets, and a missionary or two. I packed it in my hand luggage and carried it wherever I went, reading as I travelled.

Tahiti, initially, was unpleasant. The Tahitians were surly and the French imperious. Everything was expensive, not just the food, and I was embarrassed by my uncolloquial expression. My boyfriend, who was travelling with me, could speak no French at all and was as self-conscious and helpless as a child. After a couple of days on the main island we took the ferry to Moorea and got off at the wrong stop. There didn't seem to be anywhere to stay so we started walking. But as luck would have it we went the wrong way. Then it began to rain and the road turned to mud and I sat down on my calfskin suitcase and began to cry.

Night found us in a guesthouse full of insects, with threadbare sheets and peepholes through which the children watched us undress. We went in to dinner after dark and had a curious meal of marinated fish, taro, yam and some kind of stringy white fermented fruit swimming in coconut cream. When we got back to our bungalow our suitcases were gone. 'Honesty,' wrote William Wilson, first mate of the *Duff*, 'is no virtue of a South Sea islander.' Wilson came to this conclusion during a tour of the Marquesas in 1797, when some nimble-fingered local boys managed to pry the glass off the ship's compass, remove the needle and card and fit the cover back on as before. To what end no one was ever the wiser.

I went to the landlady and demanded that our suitcases be

returned, which they were, as mysteriously as they had vanished, and the entire affair was put down to a prank. The effect on our nerves, however, was deleterious, and when a coconut fell on the tin roof of our sleeping quarters in the middle of the night, I leapt out of bed, ready to fight.

The following day we moved to a compound on the other side of the island, where we paid most of the money we had left for the privilege of being treated like the rich. Suddenly there were people to talk to, tourists like ourselves, whose air of *being on holiday* had a salutary effect on our paranoia. 'I began to experience an elasticity of mind which placed me beyond the reach of those dismal forebodings to which I had so lately been a prey,' Herman Melville, also in the Marquesas, 1842.

Among our companions at the resort was a Swiss traveller who'd been wandering about the world so long he was completely serene. He was very handsome, very blond and very tan, and spent most of his time lounging about in the back garden in a pair of bathers the colour of his passport. I later discovered that he was not a real Swiss at all, but ethnically Czechoslovakian, which to my mind was significant. It is certainly true, as the anthropologist Bronislaw Malinowski once argued, that to English eyes a Slav is something like a savage. Or, to put it in more personal terms, there is a certain sexiness about Slavs and Polynesians that English and American men lack.

One night a group of us went to a nightclub in the village, where I danced provocatively with some of the boys and everyone got drunk. Then there was a fight and I escaped on the back of a motorbike, leaving my boyfriend behind in the first of what turned out to be a series of symbolic gestures. All that night I stayed up talking with the handsome Czechoslovak and at dawn we went off to have breakfast at a nearby hotel.

There are times when it seems as though you are floating about on the periphery of experience and then all of a sudden you become engaged in the most startling manner. Everything seems different. You need different things to be happy and behave differently and become a different person. Three days after the nightclub incident I told my boyfriend that I would not be getting on the plane with him in the morning. I told him that I was staying where I was and that he should go on without me.

It was, with hindsight, an astonishing decision. I had given him no real warning, perhaps some signs of minor discontent, but nothing to indicate that I was prepared to shed him like a piece of outgrown clothing. And yet that is precisely what I did. Our five long years together fell from me as carelessly as the cloth dropped by the Tahitian girl on the quarterdeck of the *Boudeuse*, the ship that brought Louis-Antoine de Bougainville to Tahiti in 1768. Thus the maiden appeared before the astonished crewmen, Bougainville wrote, 'as Venus shewed herself to the Phrygian shepherd', and the capstan 'was never hove with more alacrity'. And so it was with me. Bougainville, in a fit of French enthusiasm, named the island New Cythera after the place at which Aphrodite had risen from the sea.

From the moment the plane carrying my boyfriend left the tarmac and began its laboured ascent into the sky, my attitude toward the islands changed. No longer churlish and ill-mannered, the locals now seemed a species of the most benign humanity. Where once I had known estrangement and fear, I now found only hospitality, ease and pleasure of every innocent kind. The sun shone, the water sparkled, the rain no longer went drip-drip-drip with maddening regularity on the leaves. I no longer resented the roosters, those fiends that roam the islands like the ghosts of dead missionaries. The landscape, the people, the very air, all, as Bougainville had suggested, 'conspired to call to mind the sweets of love'.

I returned from the airport in the pre-dawn light and snuck into the bedroom of the stranger with whom I planned to pick up the thread of my romantic tale. I had not given him any indication of my plans either (if plans they were, and not improvisations), and I wasn't sure how he would take it when he found out that I had just sent my boyfriend to New Zealand so I could be there alone with him. I sat on the other bed for a little while, listening to his breathing in the darkened room, then went out and walked along the beach until it was a decent hour. Then I came back and told him over coffee.

For the next week, on an island thousands of miles from anywhere, I existed in a state of grace. I often wondered if this was what it was like for the eighteenth-century sailors, so long starved of fruit and sex and the feeling of solid land beneath their feet, when they chanced upon these tiny, jewel-like islands in the middle of this enormous sea. For a week I basked and bathed and ate and slept and made love almost continuously. It was just as the anonymous Frenchman had said in a report read by thousands of fascinated Parisiens in the 1770s: the inhabitants of these islands 'know nothing of the duration or of the origin of their existence, and, caring little about the past, concern themselves only with the present'. Though this was undoubtedly never so true of the Tahitians as it was of me.

What amuses me now, looking back, is with what relentlessness history repeats its paltry supply of scenarios. My experience in Tahiti seemed to me entirely unique, extraordinary, even freakish, a one-in-a-million sequence of events, the perfect constellation of attitudes, opportunities and chance. And yet, as I shortly discovered, European travellers to the Pacific have been acting *just like this* for over two hundred years. Think of Fletcher Christian of the *Bounty*, who ran away to Pitcairn Island with several Tahitian women in tow. Or Paul Gauguin, who traded his wife, children and metropolitan France for a shack in the shadow of an extinct volcano. Imagine how frightening this must be from the islanders' point of view: to be inundated by wanton foreigners who have abandoned all respect for propriety and think that you have too. No wonder Jean-Jacques Rousseau and Margaret Mead are so deeply resented.

The closer I look at my own experience, the more unoriginal it seems. In the space of a long tourist's week I managed to replicate the entire contact history of French Polynesia. An opening gambit marked by uneasy first encounters involving thefts and the exchange of blows – such as were experienced by Captain Samuel Wallis, the undemonstrative Englishman who discovered Tahiti for the European world – followed by the arrival of the suave and libidinous Frenchman, Bougainville, whose complete surrender to sensuous delights gave us the Polynesia of a million tourists' dreams. Such was the effect of Bougainville's report that everyone forgot about Wallis, whose first impressions of Tahiti were ambivalent at best.

When it looked to Bougainville, briefly, as though his ship might founder on the Tahitian coast, he wrote that the worst consequence of this would have been 'to exchange the sweets of the mother-country, for a peaceable life, exempted from cares'. In fact, that was not the experience of most Europeans who came and never left. They ran out of money and missed the societies they had left behind; they contracted odd diseases and often as not lived out the remainder of their lives in miserable obscurity. In the end, a remarkable number returned to the countries they had so eagerly abandoned.

For most of us, however, the question of staying on never really comes into it. We are travellers, and for us the history of islands like Tahiti is a history of both landfalls and leave-takings. Going home is on the cards from the moment of our arrival; it is what gives our visit poignancy and leads us to speculate about what it might be like never to face reality again. This is the dilemma of travel: unless one wants to finish up circling the globe like a lost explorer, the journey finally must be concluded. And so it is with many a romance, particularly one as confused with the idea of travel as this.

It was clear we could not stay in Tahiti forever. I had a ticket for New Zealand and he was bound for Fiji; then it was on to Australia for me, and Bali and Europe for him. On the night before we had to leave we talked about the future.

"Meet me in Australia," I said. "We'll go north, to Queensland. There are islands."

"Natürlich," he said, rather ambiguously.

My plane was scheduled first the following day. I said, "I'll write." He said, "I'll call." But although I have heard from him every single year since then, on my birthday, we have never again found ourselves in the same place, at the same time.

In the Restrooms of Europe

Tom Whalen

Tom Whalen is the author of *Elongated Figures*, *The Camel's Back* and *A Newcomer's Guide to the Afterlife* (with Daniel Quinn).

In the dirty restrooms of the European metropolises I saw men and men, and men and women, and women and women making love. Some, in fact, weren't actually making love, but they were thinking of making love, and for a moment I too wanted to make love, there, in the dirty bathrooms of the European metropolises. We call this condition, for lack of a better word, loneliness, though I for one wasn't lonely, more intellectually (I'm not, by the way, what anyone by any stretch of the etc. would call an intellectual) curious, though I might have been, on second thought, a little lonely, might have been feeling a bit that, a bit sexually deprived, in need of physical contact, there in the pissoirs and WCs of Europe. Yes, I might have felt an urge, a need, desire, whatever, mania, oestrus, passion, yen, zeal, appetite, avarice, nympholepsy for my flesh to smack as only flesh can against the flesh of another, it's true, there, in the waning light of a Parisian afternoon, or a Bieler morning, or a Viennese noon, to put my hand or chest or kneecaps or sexual organ on the flesh of someone who at that moment wanted also to put his etc. on someone's etc. There, in the toilets of Europe, whether graced or not with attendants, people went about their business which included making love. Or, again, if not actually making love, at least dreaming of making love in the latrines of Cologne, for there, as in the toilets of Tübingen, I saw, if not an actual sexual encounter, auras of desire around the bodies of those who wanted to make love, and perhaps one aura would someday detach itself and mingle with the aura of someone else who wanted to make love, and in that mingling of auras a third aura would arise that would bring the aura-less ones together in the urinals of European metropolises. The urinals of European metropolises are cathedrals of love, as has been noted by anyone who has ever entered one, and while I stood in a WC in Stockholm I saw a couple worshipping in their own way, and while I leaned against the wall in St Gallen I saw a young couple praying on their knees, and while I whistled in front of the latrine in Lenz I saw a man caress the sexual organ of the man next to him and noticed that no one stood next to me who might have caressed my sexual organ and felt then the previously mentioned emotion in this cathedral of Europe, this emotion that everyone must feel, I am convinced, as they enter or leave the pissoirs of Europe, these sanctuaries, fanes, basilicas of Paris, Rome, Leipzig, Oslo, Lisbon, Madrid. Children, too, must sense it, if only as a sort of future memory, but did I not also see several pairs of youngsters busy nuzzling and sucking one another in the chapels of Geneva? I did indeed. In train stations, museums, zoos, parks, airports, wherever I was in Europe I saw people wanting their sexual organs caressed, yanked, enfolded by mouth, ass and vagina. And I saw, too, in several instances, these desires being acted on. In the cathedrals of Europe, i.e., in the urinals of Europe which in every way resemble cathedrals, I saw people praying before sexual organs, or if not actually praying, then playing with the sexual organs of men and women, no matter the age. I saw old men with old men, and young women with old women, and old men with young women etc., in the restrooms of Europe, and children, too, as I've said, there in these grottoes, caves, holes, their fingers seeking out other holes in which to enter, as one enters the caves of urinals, pissoirs, WCs of Europe, whether in Konstanz or Gdansk. These monasteries, for do they not also resemble in every way monasteries, are to be found in museums, parks, movie houses, and cathedrals themselves, cathedrals within cathedrals, narthexes where sex may occur in the dark, where, it is universally recognised, it should occur. Men meet men in the public urinals of Europe, and women women, and then they come together as is often their wont, to have flesh meet flesh, so that his flesh and her flesh or her flesh and her flesh or etc. might experience the flesh of the other against one's flesh, in the urinals, where such experiences often occur, so that desires can for once be acted on, in, e.g., the toilets of Montpelier. In the WC in the Schloss of Thun, overlooked by the castle's four turrets, I stood whistling at the latrine beside a young man who was also whistling, and for a moment our whistling matched each other's. His penis was out and my penis was out, and for a moment he looked at my penis, and I in turn looked at his penis and, for a moment, we contemplated each other's penis, contemplated what it would be like if he held in his hand my prick and I in my hand his prick, what it would be like if he placed in his mouth my prick and I in turn placed in my mouth his prick, what it would be like if he located within his ass my joint, and I in turn located in my ass his joint, what it would be like, in a word, for us to come together here in this WC in Thun, beneath the gaze of the castle's four turrets. But, for better or worse, the young man turned his eyes away, and at the same time I turned my eyes, and perhaps at that moment we both experienced regret for not acting upon our desires, as I have seen so many others do in the pissoirs of the European metropolises. In these cathedrals of defecation, so to speak, I have seen women, whose faces and hands were covered with liver spots, on their knees, and I have seen children of no more than eight or nine on their knees, and I have seen men my own age on their knees worshipping, so to speak, before the altar of their dreams. The opposite of loneliness is not easy to achieve, but I have seen it done in the dirty restrooms and the clean WCs and the filthy pissoirs in every city of Europe. These grottoes of excrement and love welcome us all. A stall door opens, someone enters. Humans are a shy species. I am leaning against the wall. In the public restrooms of Europe, more so than anywhere else, it may happen that our sexual organs are stroked, caressed, licked, devoured, and for once we know happiness.

The Marriage Proposal of an Angel

from
Off the Rails

Lisa St Aubin de Terán

Lisa St Aubin de Terán was born in 1953. Her first novel, *Keepers of the House*, won the Somerset Maugham Award in 1982 and was followed by *The Slow Train to Milan* (1983) which won the John Llewellyn Rhys Prize. She has written five other novels, a collection of poetry, a collection of short stories and two memoirs of her time in Italy. She now lives in London and Italy.

I caught the ferry back to Brindisi at nine o'clock in the morning, and although this now meant that I could successfully rendezvous at Sestri Levante station at the appropriate hour to collect my son, I was very sorry to be leaving the island of Corfu so soon after discovering it. Even the most hardened tourist would admit that fifty-eight hours of travelling deserved more than an overnight stay and a crack of dawn departure.

I had stayed the night in a small balconied hotel in a beautiful balconied street bearing all the grace and elegance of a once smart French town, with alleyways of strangely oriental shops on the one side, and public gardens, a fortress and the cliffs on the other. Stavros's brother, who had a smattering of Italian, invited me to rent his house for as long as I liked, and even offered to meet my returning ferry. I took up his offer of the house, unseen, for ten days, and I found his refusal to accept any payment in advance far more binding than a cheque.

The ferry turned out to be practically full. I wandered around the available decks a couple of times, wondering where to sit for the next twelve hours, and whom to sit next to, but could not reach any decision, so I stayed leaning over the rail of the ship watching the island recede in its wake. Years before, I had sailed to Venezuela thus, leaning over the rails of the upper deck watching the sea froth and churn below me, and watching the flying fish leap through the air with their phosphorescent wings catching the sunlight in the Caribbean. This was the Adriatic, and there were no flying fish, but the feel of the railings against my midriff felt the same, and the mood that came over me was similar.

The view of Corfu kept luring my eyes towards it. The Greeks and the Romans, the eighteenth-century lords and Thomas Cook and co. were all right. It was indeed a beautiful island. And, by chance, also staring out towards its shrinking shoreline was a beautiful young man. He had the kind of beauty usually associated only with statues or pictures. There was something ethereal about the stillness of his face. The clarity of his eyes, the perfect curves and arches of his brow and chin and his large dark golden curls gave him a truly angelic aspect.

As the ferry continued to cut through the sea, and Corfu became no more than a dot on the horizon, I continued to look out while leaning over the railings. Once in a while I stole a glance at this apparition, amazed that anyone of either sex could be so physically perfect. Each time I looked, I seemed to catch his eye, and each time I caught his eye, he blushed. He could have been in his early twenties or his early thirties, it was hard to tell which, but either way he was old enough to be embarrassed to be seen to be so embarrassed. Eventually, his silent blushes drove me back into the packed inner decks of the ship.

There was, by contrast, something very squalid about the profusion of legs and elbows inside. Only a few passengers had joined the ferry at Corfu, most of them with their container lorries. The rest of the passengers had come from Piraeus, Paxos and Antipaxos, and they had been living around the tables they sat at for two days. The tourists were, again, mostly Americans, and showed signs of having come from far afield. Each table had seats for four people, and each of these already had at least two, if not three or the full quota, people and at least as many bags beside or on top of it. The whole ship was full of legs – crumpled, uncomfortable, cramped legs stretching into every available space, and all doused heavily with eggshells and stale beer and sweat.

A long-legged girl knocked into me with three cans of fizzy orange in her hands. The orange froth spilled down me, and she was recalled by her tribe in voices that implied that 'Josephine' was prone to knock into people and things, and prone also to spilling drinks. I had passed the table that she was sitting at just seconds before, and she and her companions had seemed to be slumped under the most lethal apathy. However, her return with the spilt cans enlivened them to such a degree that they began to reminisce about other occasions across Eastern Europe when drinks had been dropped and their dropping remembered. Looking back at their table, the unsteady subject of their discussion smiled apologetically at me, seraphic in this litany of her talent. In the opposite direction, where there had been stacks of luggage and one man playing Patience, there was now a cleared seat and one man playing Patience. I sat down, and he greeted me in what I now, at least, recognised as Greek.

I took out my book and read, musing on why travel had become so sordid, and why there were so many people in the world, and why so many of them were on that particular ferry, and whether Josephine Baker had ever had to dig a place for her feet under a table full of cheese-parings and peeled eggshells, and why she had taken so many children on board on her travels, and whether mine would be all right, or would I too, like her, wind up on a doorstep outside a castle evicted for debt.

The man opposite me continued to play with his cards, but, as noon approached, more and more with one eye on the barroom clock. Just before midday, he cleared the table and rummaged under the table for a long time, getting redder and redder in the face until he emerged triumphantly holding a starched white cloth which he spread over the vinyl top, and proceeded to lay for two. He made signs to me to see if I wanted to share his meal, and although I refused he continued to lay the table for two, pulling glasses and china, wine, fruit, salad, Wiener schnitzel and some pie-like things. Crowded as we were into the ship's bar, it looked incongruously elegant. One almost expected him to produce a fresh flower and make an arrangement for the centrepiece. I had just decided that I really should eat his picnic, now that he had taken so much trouble in laying it out, and was putting my book away accordingly, when Adonis from the upper deck came in, nodded to me, and squeezed in beside the other man, who turned out to be his uncle.

After much discussion between themselves, the uncle began the elaborate process of communication. It didn't take long to discover that the only language we had remotely in common was German, which he spoke with a heavy accent and I haltingly but fairly fluently as long as one didn't roam into the field of ideas. I was invited to lunch. Again I refused. They refused to eat if I didn't, so we ate together, and talked about this and that, and quickly became friends.

The uncle was a singer of Greek songs, and famous enough to have made several records, which he showed me; his nephew was a pianist. They were on their way to do a concert tour of Germany and their first concert would be in two days' time, in Frankfurt. They invited me to join them as their guest, to hear him sing. I told them I couldn't go. I had to collect my son, and now I had made plans to return to Greece. They liked the idea of my return, but were reluctant to abandon my accompanying them on their musical circuit. Sometimes they talked between themselves, the young man shy and earnest, the older very much at his ease and expansive. They seemed very fond of each other, and it was quite touching to see the deference that the nephew gave to his famous uncle and the affection that the uncle lavished on his childishly sweet nephew. After the meal we had brandies, and after the brandies we talked again.

The uncle, in particular, had a genius for separating the biographical details that I gave them into those that were genuine and those that I told them for convenience. It was as though he had a huge sieve that let the clear liquid through while keeping back the lumps. Between them they seemed to pinpoint my every weakness, and their precision made me feel uneasy. Sensing this, the uncle took out his cards, and, clearing the table, we played a Greek game that they taught me, for several hours. The game had dozens of nuances, signs and tricks that I couldn't fully grasp. After many dismal attempts to play at the same level as them, I gave up, leant back and slept.

I was awoken by the nephew, who had scarcely spoken to me, but who asked me now, in a very gentle voice, struggling with his scant knowledge of German, to stay awake because we had very little time to talk. He still wanted me to go with them to Germany. When it became clear to him that I would not, he sank his head into his hands and stayed like that for some minutes. Then he asked his uncle how many hours we had left to us, and when his uncle told him five, he groaned and retired into himself so far that he became almost invisible. Then it was his uncle's turn to plead once more for me to travel with them, and he unfolded their itinerary to me. As it turned out, they were travelling on the trans-Europe Notte, a night train to Düsseldorf that I had to take as far as Bologna. I pointed this out to him and he relaxed a little, awakening his nephew from his trance-like state to tell him that we could add six and a half more hours on to our time.

Having woken me to ask me to stay awake and talk to him, the nephew now continued to slump with his head in his hands in a state of induced coma. I wondered if he might be ill, and so asked what was the matter with him. Since he could not or would not reply, I asked his uncle, who told me.

"It has come to him, and now he is ill. He has everything, because my sister married a fine wealthy man, and he is the only son. He has his mother who loves him, but his father is dead, drowned. So he has the property of his father even though he is a young man. It is all his, a big house by the sea, so that you walk from the windows across the verandah to the water, and olive trees and grapes. And he can play the piano, always he could play the piano, as though it were not him, but something going through him. Other times, I take another pianist with me to tour, once only my nephew came. That was the best tour. He was only a boy then, but he plays best for me, and we are friends. This time he came because I am tired, and getting a little older now, so it tires me to tour. He will look after me, he is good and kind. Only now he wants to turn back if you do not come. He wants you to come. It has come to him and it can never go away. All the villages around where he lives know him. Look at him, he is beautiful. All the girls see him, tall and still, and they love him. He takes them out for an evening, a day, and then . . . finish."

Here the uncle dusted his hands as though dispatching the hordes of eager maidens from him.

"Never, never, do the girls go back to his house. Never. Now it has come to him. He wants to marry you, he wants you to go back to his island, take his house, all that he has, my nephew loves you. He asks you to marry him. He is afraid you will go. He is sick in his heart."

I couldn't think of a single thing to say to this second-hand proposal. On the one hand it was utterly ridiculous; on the other it was so bizarre that I found it alarmingly attractive. In a great gesture of cowardice I excused myself and went to the loo, where I stayed for the best part of half an hour. Things have to be pretty serious to stay in a ship's bathroom for that long, but I was feeling upstaged. I was Miss Impulsive, or, rather, Mrs Impulsive, since I had now, nominally, been married for fifteen years in all. Suddenly *I* was becoming the voice of caution, the hanger-back. I went out and up on deck and took up my position over the railings, looking into the sea to find out what the troubled spume had to say about all these goings on. They seemed to beat out a message which was loud and clear in whatever language one spoke. I had married my first husband because he was beautiful and mysterious and had asked me to out of the blue and then insisted. He also suffered so deeply when I turned him down that I ultimately accepted, if only to save him from such pain and grief. It had taken me nine years to extricate myself from that marriage, and who knew how many more to recover from the loneliness of being married to and living with a complete stranger.

The nephew came up behind me, touched my shoulder, and then stood beside me, leaning over the railings too. I don't know what the waves were telling him, or, indeed, if he was listening to them, but they kept on pounding out the same message to me, defining it now as five simple words beating in against the ship's side: *Leave the train at Bologna.*

We arrived in Brindisi just as we had left Corfu, with the two of us watching the sea, while I simultaneously watched the mainland and stole odd glances at him, which made him blush; and he stared strangely at me, feeling, I felt, either sick in his heart or sick in his head.

*

At the beginning of its journey along the Adriatic coast, the night train through Europe's only concession to the idea of long-distance travel is the names that it slots on to the sides of its carriages. Inside, the train is just the usual string of compartments, a few of which convert into untended bunks, but many of which don't. Outside, it is like a great articulated gecko in a dusty blue skin, disjointing itself through the night and discarding the bits. So one carriage will be shunted away to Copenhagen, another to Amsterdam, another to Spain, to Turkey, to France, to Switzerland, and the small remaining vital core will eventually find its way to Düsseldorf, hence its subtitle of the Düsseldorf Express.

Its passengers at Brindisi are mostly from the incoming ferries. Out of season, these dock only on alternate days, so there are, accordingly, alternate days when the Düsseldorf Express starts its journey relatively empty. In the holiday season, when the ferries sail in daily to the port of Brindisi and unload what look like impossibly large loads of passengers who emerge from its bowels like a steaming human froth, the Düsseldorf Express is correspondingly and nightmarishly full.

Its passengers range from the disbelieving to the discontented to the incensed. More than any other train in Europe, it seems to give one a sense of being cheated. People try to charge it under the trade descriptions act. Travelling nowadays across the Channel, people seem to have become resigned to the fact that there is scarcely ever a restaurant car across France on the trains from Boulogne and Calais. If there is, one is pleasantly surprised. If there isn't, the small hamper comes into its own. Then again, I have seen people disappointed by the absence of any drinking water on these trains, and, at times, even gasping in the night for something to drink. But the name fits the train. Thus the boat train doesn't drop people in the middle of Leeds, or on the inland parts of the Kent countryside, it takes them to a boat, or at worst, the dock where they can catch one. And the Naples Express, the 210 of which I am so fond, is fast, if little else, and does come and go to Naples. The train that goes from Calais to Milan Central pretends to do nothing else: it is not advertised as the Gourmet Special, or the Bistro Bonanza, so one arrives in Milan without the sense of having been taken, so to speak, for a ride. Right from the start, before there has even been so much as a shunting from the station, the Düsseldorf Express looks as though it were wearing a disguise.

A couple of hundred tourists have been funnelled off the ferry and have marched, as though in a demonstration, up the main street of Brindisi, with backpacks for placards. They show every sign of having survived arduous and intrepid experiences. Enamel mugs and coffee-pots hang ostentatiously from the straps of their voluminous luggage. They give the impression sometimes of having spent much of their travels trying to stamp some outward mark of the places they have been to on their persons. So they also wear Tibetan caps, tonsured hair, fakir-length fingernails and a number of other cosmetic tricks ranging from views of the Taj Mahal tattooed on their cheeks to discarded python skins wrapped around their necks. All this is meant to give the clear impression that they have just returned like so many Marco Polos from the East. Their luggage has often become huge ethnic baskets instead of backpacks. They have ways of making you believe that they have come from India (whether in fact they have or not). The image is all-important. Perhaps that is why the disappointment is so immense when the train that is to bear them back to their despised ones is so uncivilised.

Just as it is the Americans, with their long legs and their transatlantic confidence, who stride ahead through the town, so it is the Americans who tend to take the lead in their disapproval of the train. When they are in the desert (man), they can just lie out on sand under the stars; but when a train calls itself an international express, it should at least look like one.

Passengers are coaxed in by the guards, who try hard to persuade them that all is well and that, despite its provincial appearances, this train really will take them to Copenhagen, or Amsterdam, or Geneva. Some people, particularly the older ones, just refuse to board it, believing that there must be a better one if only they wait. So they do just that, only to find that Brindisi is a long way from anywhere, especially by night, and, unwillingly, that their only alternative is to wait until the next evening and catch the same thing and follow the same route, but with the extra bitterness of having their European programme thrown out by twenty-four hours.

The real trouble begins after the train leaves the station. While it is still at the platform, the guards can say that it really is an express. Once it begins to crawl through the night, practically bump-starting at every out-of-the-way station along the Adriatic coast and then creeping inland, like a sick centipede, on its way to Bologna, there is no avoiding the deceit. It is night, and the places have strange names and desolate platforms. The corridors vibrate to the complaints of travellers hijacked by the night. People are tortured by the pace. Many a clogged artery clogs a little more as the Düsseldorf Express creeps through the Italian night, moving sometimes no faster than a decrepit old man, crippled and limping on ill-fitting artificial limbs.

Gradually, as bits of the original train are disconnected at the most unlikely stations, and proper carriages from other trains are linked up to the skeleton, the snail to Düsseldorf takes on at least the semblance of a proper express, even though it continues to feel its way through the night. At Bologna, it waits for an hour, during which time it breaks out of its maggoty chrysalis, emerging into the darkness of Reggio Emilia a fully winged creature to speed its way on through the Alps. I was to leave the train at Bologna. I had to leave the train at Bologna. All the way there, I reminded myself of this, because all the way there, much more than on the boat, I felt myself being swept off my feet.

As the nephew and I had followed the procession of passengers up the main street of Brindisi, his uncle had darted on ahead to procure seats. The sense of being borne by the crowd was so overpowering that it made me feel silly, as did my walking beside this man who insisted on considering himself engaged to be married, and who was a little out of sorts because of the failure, on my part, to sort out the terms of the agreement. Then a bar seemed to beckon to me as we passed its open door, and I dived in, quickly followed by the staggeringly beautiful, but very confused, nephew.

It flashed through my mind, for the first time, that although we were such excellent friends now, the Greek musicians and I, and although I fully intended to disembark at Bologna, there was the chance that they might not let me. I didn't know. It all seemed a bit far-fetched, and I doused the thought with a double brandy. Through the bottom of my glass I spied a familiar face entering the bar, quickly followed by another. These were two of the three men I had met, lunched with, drunk with, and been shown the not inconsiderable sights of the city of Brindisi by, on my way through to Greece, just three days before. I had forgotten their kindness in escorting me to the ferry, and also their equally kind offer of meeting the ferries back the following week to have a drink and take me to my train with a proper and fitting farewell. I was just rummaging around in my brain for a suitable apology and trying to organise an introduction, furnish an explanation and invite them to join us, when the epitome of human beauty solved the problem for me by intimating through some very expressive facial movements that both of the two newcomers could scram. They looked at me, counting on me, I saw, to introduce them for what they were: friendly dolphins and not sharks. I stood up to do so, reaching out my hand to shake theirs. The nephew also rose to his feet and, stepping between me and the newcomers with the agility of a dancer but the ferocity of a wolverine, caused them to leave me mid-sentence, while the proprietorial pianist muttered something about there being no time.

The Greek uncle had found a compartment of his own, and having laid out a dinner for three on his damask napery he was leaning through the window, looking out for the happy couple-to-be. The train left late, as it often does, due to the grumbling and harassment of its human cargo, and shuddered out of old Brindisium with a series of spasmodic jerks.

Christ may have stopped at Eboli, but the guidebooks all stopped before Brindisi, leaving it with its ferries and its Roman remains stranded inside its palings of peach and almond blossoms, and peaches and almonds themselves, with its secrets kept and its spirits unspoiled. Shunting through the spectral empty stations of the Adriatic coast in the middle of the night and the small hours of the morning grants the passing tourist no impression of the wild beauty of the dunes and the savage hills behind them. Bari and Foggia, Termoli and Vasto are just names in the night, and a sleepless one at that. Even places like Pescara, where the poet d'Annunzio was born, or Ancona, with its high cathedral built on the site of the temple of Venus, pass unnoticed. Rossini's Pesaro holds no arias; and Rimini, the littered cluttered villain of that coast, slides by under the same anonymous blanket as everywhere else on the line.

All through the heavily veiled Molise and the equally impenetrable Abruzzi, my marriage to the nephew and my Greek future were discussed in pidgin German. Neither of them would accept my adamant refusal. "We are in the hands of destiny," they told me, and I had no choice. I remembered the windy bus-stop on the edge of Clapham Common where my first husband had proposed to me, and I remembered that he too had called it *la fuerza del destino*. One had to be careful of destiny; she has a lot to answer for.

"You don't need to love him," the uncle insisted in his strange German dialect. "He loves you."

The discussion was endless, and endlessly repetitive. I dragged in Iseult and Alexander as blocking pawns, but the nephew loved children. He had never seen them, I said. He didn't need to, I was told, he had seen me, and that was enough. I dragged in the madness of my family, and its total unsuitability as a credential for marriage. I threw enough sand on the scheme to have flattened the dunes from Brindisi to Otranto. The nephew, who had never wanted to marry before, wanted to marry me, now. I told him a hundred times, if I told him once, that I was already married. They would pay for my divorce, they would pay for my upkeep and that of my children and the seven imaginary sisters that I had invented in place of my three actual ones. Money was no problem. I was being brainwashed into believing nothing was a problem. The more tender and emotional they became, the more I felt that I might have a real problem trying to get off the train: an emotional holocaust was brewing, and I was to blame.

Had I not absolutely had to meet young Alexander by a given hour that day, I would have jumped the train at Pescara when it stopped there and cut short the flaying of the nephew's nerves. However, I had promised to arrive, and left it too late to make a later rendezvous, so I had no choice but to catch my connection at Bologna. The train stopped for a long time at Pescara, over an hour, and the distraught uncle went in and out to the corridor to smoke. In between their joint entreaties to me, mostly voiced through the senior partner, they had fierce whispered arguments in Greek. It seemed that the nephew was refusing to go to Germany if I insisted on leaving the train at Bologna. I could see it was a good ploy; it had worked for lunch, why not now?

The uncle was in the corridor under a great halo of Karelia smoke. His beatific nephew was sitting opposite me invoking the god of destiny by repeating, 'Kommst du mit mir' in what sounded like a slowed down Gregorian chant.

Then, quite unexpectedly, he said, in English, "Are you with me?"

Not a word of English had been spoken all day or night. Perhaps that was all he knew, conjured up from some advertisement or remembered phrase. The train pulled out of Pescara at that moment, reminding me of its satyric, illustrious and eccentric son, Gabriele d'Annunzio. Marching to take Fiume after the First World War, with a band of rebel soldiers all ready to die, he had said, "Those who are not with me are against me."

As we crawled back into the night, leaving the dimly lit station behind us, the words seemed to take on a curious, almost sinister connotation. The train lurched, and the sliding door to our compartment slid shut. Looking up, I caught a glimpse of the nephew's eyes; they were hurt and flickering with something that looked like anger. I felt afraid, with an indefinable fear. I began to watch him closely now, avoiding his eyes. He pulled out a bag from under his seat with the heels of his feet, and then, still watching me, he plunged his hand inside it, bringing out a broad twelve-inch knife. I watched it with dread. It was double-edged. He held it for a moment, saying nothing, but with his knuckles clenched so tightly round the blade that they went white. In my mind, I had already died.

Five years before, in Paris, someone had tried to strangle me. I fainted then and escaped with only a necklace of bruises round my neck and a phobia about even the gentlest touch on my throat. At the time of the strangling, I realised, some seconds before it happened, that that was what was in the air. I had felt the same chill numb terror as I felt now. I was overwhelmed by my own idiocy, and I felt a pain in my lungs at the thought of my two children, followed by a smell of mimosa which was to blossom in six weeks' time.

Then he took out an apple and began to slice it, and offered me a sliver, which I took, trying not to let him see how much my hands were shaking. I moved across to the far corner of the compartment, near the door, and pretended to sleep.

He continued to play with his knife, stroking the blade and staring with an expression of crazed innocence on his face. I stole glances at him, but felt intuitively that if I said the wrong thing, he'd stab me. After what seemed like many minutes, he picked up his apple again, and continued to eat it. The moment seemed to have passed, whatever it was, and I, drained by my recent fear and the adrenaline that had pumped round my body in the last three minutes, reasoned that if he was going to kill me, I'd rather he did it in my sleep; and if he wasn't, I was tired anyway.

I woke to see a dimly lit sign announcing our arrival at a place

LISA ST AUBIN DE TERÁN

called Civitanova. The nephew was sitting beside me, his uncle stretched out across three seats in front. His grasp of German seemed a lot better than it had been all day, as though he had either been practising while I slept, or his mind had simply cleared in the interval. He asked me not to sleep, but to take pity on his pain, and he asked me not to agree to a marriage but at least to promise to go to Germany within the week to see him. I agreed to both these things, and he was so pleased he wept. Although he didn't know it, I would have agreed to practically anything by then.

I come from a totally paranoid family. My grandmother was so paranoid that she believed in a world conspiracy to undo her, like a piece of knitting that life was unravelling on a daily basis. My mother was paranoid, my sisters are paranoid, my daughter is paranoid – even my two-year-old son was paranoid. We all think we are being watched. In our calmer moments we realise and accept that we actually are being watched, or rather noticed, and this contributes and possibly creates that constant sense of surveillance. I cannot bear to walk in the dark with anyone behind me, just as I cannot bear to drive, day or night, with another car behind me. Most of the time, I can talk myself out of my uneasiness and let it pass. But having been half strangled once, kidnapped once, and attacked a couple of times, when I feel a real sense of threat I follow my tardy instincts and become as spinelessly accommodating as the situation demands. Had the uncle been a priest or judge, I would have become a bigamist then and there if I felt that it increased my chances of leaving the compartment in one piece.

For the two hundred kilometres from Ancona to Bologna the nephew sat beside me, showing no signs of violence, no restless fingers, no wires or blades. He asked me to hold his hand, which

I did, and was strangely comforted by his touch. After Rimini he cried silently, some of his tears finding their way on to the inside of my wrist. At Casena he awakened his uncle and whispered to him in Greek, whereupon his uncle rummaged in his coat and produced a notebook, address book and a pen. He wrote out some half a dozen addresses and telephone numbers in Frankfurt, explaining who each person was and how to arrive at the place or leave a message. They had already given me their Greek addresses, but he gave them to me again, adding those of cousins and neighbours to enable me to arrive there if need be. Then he slept again, I think more out of genuine exhaustion than any desire to leave us on our own. The nephew's head had long been leaning on my shoulder. As the train rocked into Bologna, I realised that he was sleeping too.

I got up, took my miniature suitcase and opened the door practically in one movement. They awoke, the nephew tumbling into the space where my shoulder had been. The bright lights and the noise on the platform outside spoke for themselves. They said nothing, and neither did I. I held my hand up as a token farewell, and left. Once on the platform I hurried towards the steps that would lead me away. I was aware, without looking, that they had come to the window. I felt their presence over my head as I walked by. Before I reached the steps I heard my name called, and then again. The second call reminded me of the strangled cry of a woman in Venezuela at the moment when her dead son was carried out in his coffin. I walked on. It came again, alarming all the other passengers, who turned to look. Then I turned back, guided by a surge of memory and emotion to where they hung leaning from the window.

The uncle was crying for his nephew, the nephew was weeping for himself, and I was crying too, I don't know why or for whom. I gave my suitor back the hand that I had stolen from him in the train, and he held it until all the blood drained out of my arm raised to meet his.

The whistles blew, and the uncle made me promise again to come to Frankfurt, which I did, knowing that I wouldn't go.

"If you don't come, in two weeks we come to find you," he said, and I smiled, feeling lousy, but safe in having given them the wrong address in Liguria. As the whistles blew, I saw only their kindness and concern and the really astonishing beauty of my new fiancé.

The whistles blew again, and the guard with the red luminous lollipop waved the train out of the station. The gathering motion wrenched our fingers apart, scattering tears over mine. I had two hours to wait until my next train. It took me a while to stop crying, and then I slept, fitfully, in the bleak waiting room, thinking, each time I woke, that they had both been right in a way, when they called it destiny, for it was my destiny to be loved by strangers.

from
The Lady and the Monk

Pico Iyer

Pico Iyer is a longtime essayist for *Time*, and his pieces appear regularly in the *TLS*, the *New York Review of Books* and many magazines on both sides of the Atlantic and the Pacific. His books include *Video Night in Kathmandu*, *Falling Off the Map*, *Cuba and the Night* and, most recently, *Tropical Classical*. He now lives in Japan with the heroine of his *Lady and the Monk*.

Oone delicate autumn day a few days later – the sky now grey, now blue, always like a woman's uncertain heart, a light drizzle falling, and then subsiding, and falling once more – I met Sachiko outside an Indonesian store, for a trip to Kurama. She was, as ever, girlishly dressed, her hair falling thickly over one side of her face, held back on the other by a black comb with a red stone heart in its middle; the tongues of her black sneakers hanging out from under lime-green legwarmers.

As we travelled towards the hillside village, she set down her backpack beside her on the train and began telling me excitedly about her friend Sandy, and how it was Sandy who had first introduced her to Zen, Sandy who had first taken her to a temple, Sandy who had first encouraged her to try *zazen* meditation. "I Japanese," she said softly. "But I not know my country before. Sandy my teacher." More than that, she said, it was Sandy who had shown her another way of life and given her the confidence to try new things. Sandy, supporting two children alone in a foreign country and at the same time embarked on a full-length course of Zen studies, had shown her that it was possible, even for a woman, to have a strong heart.

Now, she went on, Sandy was planning to send her children back to America for high school. "I dream, maybe Hiroshi go your country, Sandy's son together. You see this movie *Stand by Me*?" I nodded. "Very beautiful movie. I want give my son this life. I dream, he little *Stand by Me* world feeling." And what about her husband's view on all this? An embarrassed giggle. "I don't know. Little difficult. But I much dream children go other

75

country." She paused, deep in thought. "But I also want children have Zen spirit inside, Japanese feeling." I asked her to explain. "Example – you and Sandy, *zazen* very difficult. Japanese people, *zazen* very easy. I want my children have this spirit."

"But if your children go away, they may grow distant. Maybe never talk to you. Maybe forget all Japanese things. Wouldn't that make you sad?"

"*Tabun.* Maybe."

"It's very difficult, I think."

And so we get off the train, and climb from shrine to shrine, scattered across the steep hills of Kurama, and the rain now drizzles down, now stops again, and the two of us huddle under her umbrella, sweaters brushing, her hair almost falling on my arm. "*Ai to ai gasa,*" I say, thinking of the phrase I had read in a Yosano Akiko poem, describing two people sharing a single umbrella. "Maybe," she says, with a lilting laugh, and we climb some more, the hills before us resplendent now, and then still higher, in the gentle rain, till we are sitting on a log.

In front of us, the trees are blazing. "I like colour now," she says, pensive. "Later, I not so like. More sad. Leaves die. Many thing change." And then, carried away by the view, perhaps, she recalls the only other time she has come to this hill. Kurama is only a few miles north of Kyoto, a thirty-minute train ride. But Sachiko has not been here for fifteen years, and all that time, she says, she has longed to return. "I so happy," she whispers, as if in the presence of the sacred. "I so excited. Thank you. Thank you very much. I very happy. Very fun. Before I coming here, little teenage size, together three best friend. We climbing mountain, I very afraid, because I thinking snake. Much laughing, many joke. Very fun. My friends' names, Junko, Sumiko and Michiko. But Osaka now. Very busy, marry ladies."

We walk down again, through the drizzle and the mist, then up slippery paths, between the trees. "I much love Kurama," she says quietly, as if in thought. "Sometimes I ask husband come here; he say, 'You always want play. I very busy. I cannot.' And come here together children, very difficult. Soon tired. Thank you very much, come here this place with me."

This is all rather sad. She tells me of her adventures, and the smallness of it all makes me sad again: how, when she was a little girl, she went with her cousin and brother and aunt to a cinema, and her aunt allowed her to go and see *The Sound of Music* alone. "I very scared. All dark. Many person there. But then, film begin, I soon forget. I much love. I dream I Julie Andrews." She also describes reading about Genghis Khan. "I dream I trip together Genghis Khan. I many trip in my heart, many adventure. But only in my heart." She tells me how once, last year, for the first time ever, she went alone to Osaka, forty minutes away, to see the Norwegian teenybopper group a-ha in concert, and then, exhilarated by this event, went again that same week to another of their concerts, in Kobe, with her son and her cousin, all three of them sharing a room in a luxury hotel. The night she spent in the hotel, the trip to the coffee shop after the concert, the way she had chanced to see the lead singer's parents in the coffee shop and then to meet the star himself in an elevator – all live on in her as what seems almost the brightest moment in her life. "I very lucky. I very excited. I dream, maybe next summer, I go this hotel again. See other a-ha concert."

And when she says, more than once, "I live in Kyoto all life; you come here only one month, but you know more place, very well," I feel again, with a pang, a sense of the tightly drawn limits of a Japanese woman's life, like the autumn paths vanishing in mist around us. For I could see that she was saying something

77

more than the usual "Tourists know more of towns than their residents ever do," and I could catch a glimpse of the astonishing circumscription of her life. Even while her brother had been to Kansas City to study for three years and was now in his third year of pursuing Jung in Switzerland, she had never really been outside Kyoto. She now worked two mornings a week in a doctor's office, but it was the same place where she had worked during junior high school and high school, in vacations, just around the corner from her parents' house. Her cousin, a kind of surrogate sister, sometimes worked in the same place. Her own house was in the next neighbourhood down, within walking distance of her parents-in-law's house. And her mother still called her every night, to see how she was doing.

Every year, she said, her husband got three or four days of holiday, and the trips the family took together on these breaks – to the sea once, and once to Tokyo Disneyland – still lived within them as peak experiences. Even a trip such as the one today, for a few hours to a suburb, seemed a rare and unforgettable adventure.

"Please tell me your adventure," she begins to say. "Please tell me other country. I want imagine all place," but I don't know where to begin, or how to convey them to someone who has never been in a plane, and what cloak-and-dagger episodes in Cuba, or nights in the Thai jungle, will mean to one who has scarcely left Kyoto.

"I dream you life-style," she goes on, as if sensing my unease. "You are bird, you go everywhere in world, very easy. I all life living only Kyoto. So I dream I go together you. I have many, many dream in my heart. But I not have strong heart. You very different."

"Maybe. I was lucky that I got used to going to school by

plane when I was nine."

"You very lucky. I afraid other country. Because I thinking, maybe I go away, my mother ill, maybe die. If I come back, maybe no mother here." Her mother, she explains, developed very serious allergies – because, it seemed, of the new atmospheric conditions in Japan. (All this I found increasingly hard to follow, in part because Sachiko used 'allergy' to mean 'age' – she regularly referred to the 'Heian allergy', and when she was talking about 'war allergy', I honestly didn't know if it was a medical or a historical point she was making. I, of course, was no better, confusing *sabishii* with *subarashii*, and so on, in trying to say, "Your husband must be lonely," invariably coming out with, "Your husband is wonderful. Just fantastic," which left her frowning in confusion more than ever.)

"When I little children size, my mother many times in hospital. And Grandma too. And when my brother in Kansas City, my grandma die. He never say goodbye. She see my husband, she think he my brother. Very sad time. So I always dream in heart, because many sad thing happen. But dream stay in heart." This seemed a sorrowful way to approach the universe, though eminently pragmatic. Yet she held to it staunchly. "Maybe tomorrow I have accident. I die. So I always keep dream." That was lovely, elegant, Sachiko: Sachiko, in her teenager's high-tops, keeping a picture of Sting in her wallet and sometimes losing sleep over him – a thirty-year-old girl with daydreams.

All this gets us onto what is fast becoming a recurrent theme in our talks, the competing merits of the Japanese and the American family systems. I, of course, argue heartily for the Japanese.

"It makes me so happy to see mothers and children playing together here, or going to temples together, and movies, and coffee shops. In America, mothers and daughters are often strangers. People do not know their parents, let alone their grandparents. Sometimes, in California, parents just fly around, with very young girlfriends or boyfriends, and leave their children with lots of money but no love." (My sense of America, in Japan, was getting as simplistic and stereotyped as my sense of Japan had been in America.) "So fifteen-year-old girls have babies and drive cars, and have money, many boyfriends and lots of drugs."

"Maybe. But in your country, I think, children have strong heart. Do anything, very easy. Here in Japan, no strong heart. Even grown-up person, very weak!" I think she means that they lack adventure, recklessness and freedom, and in all that I suppose she is right, and not only because twelve Japanese CEOs have literally collapsed this year under the pressures of a strong yen. And she, of course, as a foreigner, sees only the pro ledger in America, while I, over here, stress only the con – though when I am in America, I find myself bringing back to American friends an outsider's sense of their country's evergreen hopefulness.

And as we continue walking, a few other people trudge past us up the hill, elders most of them, with sticks, the men in berets and raincoats, the women in print dresses, occasionally looking back through the curtain of fine drizzle at the strange sight of a pretty young Japanese girl with a shifty Indian male. Sachiko, however, seems lost in another world.

"What is your blood type?" she suddenly asks, eyes flashing into mine.

"I don't know."

"True?"

"True."

"Whyyy?" she squeals, in the tone of a high school girl

seeking a rock star's autograph.

"I don't know. In my country, people aren't concerned about blood types."

"But maybe you have accident. Go hospital."

"I don't know."

"Really? True??"

"Really. Foreigners think it's strange that the Japanese are so interested in blood types."

"Really? *Honto ni*?"

"Yes." I am beginning to feel I am letting her down in some way, so I quickly ask if she is interested in the Chinese calendar, or astrology. All this, though, is frightful to try to translate, and when Sachiko says that she is the sign of the 'ship' and I say, "Ah yes, you mean the waves," she looks very agitated. "No, no waves! Ship!" Now it's my turn to look startled. What is going on here? "The Water Bearer?" "No." "The Fish?" "No. Ship!" She is sounding adamant. Then, suddenly, I recall that Aries is the ram. (Thank God, I think, for all those years in California!) "Oh – sheep! You are the sheep sign." "Yes, Ship."

And then, of a sudden, she plops down on a bench, and draws out from her backpack a Japanese edition of Hesse, and shows me the stories she likes, and repeats how he had struck a chord in her when young. "When I little high school size, I much much like. But Goldmund, not so like. When I twenty, it not so touch my heart, not same feeling. Now thirty, maybe different feeling. Which you like?"

"I don't know. That's why I'm reading it again now. When I was young, I liked Goldmund. Then, later, I understood Narziss a little better. For a long time, I spent one month living like Goldmund, travelling around the world, and one month like Narziss, leading a monk's life at home. Now I'm trying both at the same time, to see which one is better."

Somehow the world has misted over as we talk, and time and space are gone: the world, I think, begins and ends on this small bench. And as we sit there, sometimes with her dainty pink umbrella unfurled, sometimes not, I pointing to the yellow trees, or the blue in the sky, and saying, "*Onna-no kokoro, Kurama-no tenki*" (The weather in Kurama is like a woman's heart), I can see her perfect white teeth when she laughs, the mole above her lips, a wisp of hair across her forehead, another fine strand that slips into her ear. She bends over to look at the magazine in my hands, and her hair falls all about me.

"You tell parent about girlfriend?" she says, looking up.

"Well, for many years, I haven't had – or wanted – a girlfriend."

"So what am I?" A long silence. "I man?" She giggles girlishly, and I don't know where that puts us: our discourse is soft and blurred as autumn rain.

"I think you're a very beautiful lady," I say, looking down at my outstretched legs like a bashful schoolboy. "Your husband is a very lucky man."

"I not so think. I bad wife."

And then, seizing the closeness in the air, she tries to formulate more complex thoughts. "I very happy. Today, time stop. Thank you very much, coming here this place together me. I only know you short time, but you best friend feeling. I think I know you long time. I no afraid, no weak heart. You foreigner man, but I alone together you, very easy. I think maybe you very busy man. But talking very easy. I very fun, thank you." All of this is a little heartbreaking, I think, together on a bench on a misty autumn day, and she so excited to see me after only two weeks of acquaintance.

Standing up, we start walking slowly down the hill, through faint drizzle, talking of her closeness to her mother, and the poems of Yosano Akiko. And as we leave the hill of temples behind us, she turns and bows towards the shrine, pressing her palms together and closing her eyes very tight.

That evening, I read Yosano Akiko late into the night and try to recall the short *tanka* Sachiko had recited to me on the hill. But I know only that it begins with *kimi*, the intimate form of 'you', as so many of Akiko's poems do. Falling asleep over the book, I awaken with a start in the dead of night, imagining that I am holding her by the hand and saying, "Sachiko-san, I'm sorry to disturb you. I know you have a husband, and I'm very sorry, but . . ."

And later in the night, I think of the two of us under her pink umbrella, and flip hurriedly through the book in search of the phrase '*ai to ai gasa*'. When I find it, my heart seems almost to stop: it is, it seems, a classic image of intimacy, and one of the most famous figures in Japan for lovers.

Piranha

Maureen Stanton

Maureen Stanton is an American writer whose essays have appeared in *Creative Nonfiction* and *The Sun*. She has also published a series of columns in *Comic Relief* and *Funny Times*.

Y ou cannot drive to Iquitos, Peru, a city that once exported more rubber for automobile tyres than any other in the world. The city is a prisoner of the Andes mountains. Access is by plane or by boat up the Amazon River. We arrive by plane, from Miami, via Lima.

Once in Iquitos, our guides, Angel and Roldan, help us onto a thatch-roofed skiff and we motor three hours down the Amazon to our camp on a tributary, the Rio Negro. As we make our way down river, chunks of the bank fold into the water and huge palms belly flop and drift like tiny branches in the swift current. It is the middle of the rainy season and the water is high.

When we arrive, people scatter to nap in hammocks. Angel invites me to ride in the dugout. He is a sombre man, with smouldering good looks: angular jaw, high broad forehead, pronounced cheekbones, and smooth skin the colour of the muddy water. He paddles until we are alone, dives overboard, and treads water.

"How about we play I be the piranha and you be the bait."

I dip my finger in the silty water and he bites it. I become nervous, my finger in his mouth.

"Take me back," I say.

As we walk up the path toward the huts he says, "Meet me at ten tonight."

∗

Dinner is rice, red beans, and fish just pulled from the water, wrapped in banana leaves and roasted over hot coals.

Mangoes for dessert.

"I show you how to eat a mango," Angel says. He halves the fruit and makes a cross-hatch into the flesh with his sharp pocket knife. He inverts it and neat, divided squares pop up like buildings in a city. I bite into the pulp, and he reaches over and licks a drop of carrot-coloured juice from my wrist.

At ten o'clock, when Angel has asked me to meet him, I am under gauzy mosquito netting safe from bites in the night.

*

On Tuesday morning we cruise down the river. I feel the splash of the Amazon cool on my backside as I pee in a hopper mounted over the engine. We dive off the boat and swim with pink dolphins, which in legend make love to women who then give birth to otherworldly creatures that cannot live on land or in water. The guides heave us back into the boat like big white fish.

That afternoon we hike in the jungle. I stumble over roots as I look around. Everything is oversized, the jungle a humid, dense womb. I recognise philodendron, a house plant, except here it is fifty feet tall and makes me feel Lilliputian. Leaves are the size of my body. I want to lie down in one and fold it around me like a blanket. Katydids are as big as my hand. Huge, thousand-year-old trees – kapok, mahogany – rise from buttresses three cars wide, space you can live in.

In the canopy the oropendula, a bird of liquid gold, drips its call onto the jungle floor. Monkeys mock us, glide through the treetops like it is another dimension. I nearly squash a poison arrow frog the size of a marble, orange and deadly. Roldan slashes at a rubber tree with his machete. We touch the milk as it oozes out, viscous, pearly.

After dinner we head to the bar for cold beer. I can feel Angel looking at me. I am dirty, pale, patchy with insect bites. I perspire industriously, my hair wrapped in a wet knot. I drink one beer, then another waiting for something to happen. I return to my hut, but can't sleep because of the heat. In the distance I hear a drum beat.

*

It is drizzling at dawn but it feels cool and good as we chug along the shore. Angel and Roldan point to specks flying through the air and flashes in the foliage. Yellow-headed cara cara and blue crowned motmot. Several people in the group become wildly excited.

"Ornithology alert!" one man says, binoculars poised. Angel's vision is acute from boyhood days of hunting monkey and jaguar. He spots a sloth fifty yards up a tree that I swear is a burl until it inches upward.

We return for breakfast. Scrambled eggs and bread, dense, succulent bananas and pineapples, and thick, yellowish, sweet star-fruit juice. Afterward, we hike deep into the jungle. Angel stalks a butterfly, catches it by its wings which are perfectly clear, like windows, and strokes its thorax until it is enervated, hypnotised. We catch sight of an erratically flying butterfly, iridescent, like a piece of shiny taffeta. A blue morpho. We hush as it rhapsodises into the canopy.

At a small pond we climb into shallow, tipsy dugouts. The guides' smooth, sinewy biceps stroke water so black you cannot see into it, an onyx mirror, a lake of oil. We glide inches from electric eels, caiman and piranha. Hoatzins, claw-winged birds as ancient as dinosaurs and big as chickens, perch heavily in boughs above us while bats swoop and dive bomb over our heads. We drift into giant lily pads, chartreuse carpets the size of bathtubs. I want to leap out and lie on one the same way I have the urge to jump out the window of an airplane and float on cottony clouds. Angel lifts the lily pad with his oar. Its pink underside is delicate and fleshy, naked. I want to bite it, to feel it, to rub my body against its texture. I drink in the beauty of the guides, their stone hard thighs, as they carry the dugouts over their heads and lead us back to camp.

*

When we return, Angel invites me for a swim. He paddles us into a thicket of mangroves, past a man fishing for piranha.

"They taste sweet," he says.

"How can we swim here with piranha?"

"They just do like this." He pinches my arm lightly. His fingers rest there.

"They attack if there is a lot of blood," he says. We get out of the dugout and hang onto a protruding branch. Angel kisses me. I pull away just as the fisherman strokes by. On our way back, Angel steers toward a woman scrubbing clothes in the river.

"You want to wash your hair?"

I stand in the water, mud swallowing my ankles, as Angel circles his fingers on my scalp. We paddle back to camp, past catfish crawling out of the water up the banks to their holes. Fish that walk on land, prehistoric, futuristic, creatures of two worlds.

*

After dinner, the single women from our group go to the bar. The guides play guitar, bongos and flute.

"Malagueña," Roldan sings, his voice like warm grey coals. The air pulses with the sounds of mosquitoes, crickets, frogs. We dance with the guides, slow, smooth, close.

The night moves away and the women slowly, dreamily, go back to their rooms. Angel walks past me, and whispers, "Meet me." Back under my netting I am waiting for the time to arrive. Fixed time in the jungle seems odd. Everything moves, vibrates, grows so fast that the guides have to machete the trails every other day. I steal down the path toward the far end of the camp where the guides sleep. I hear a whisper from the bushes. Angel leads me to an empty hut. We are silent as we lift the netting and lie together on the mattress.

His lips are sweet. I buff my tongue across them to taste the sweetness, and he presses his body against mine. I am white, ghostly, glowing. He moves his mouth over my body.

"I show you how to eat a mango," he says.

The next day we visit a village that is celebrating the rains. Men and women parade around a pole, stagger, sleep on the ground. Children squat to pee on the grass. Angel takes me over to an old woman sitting cross-legged in a corner. He scoops up some lumpy, white, yeasty liquid from a pot near her and offers it to me to drink. "Masata," Angel says, "from manioc." Women chew the roots for days and spit them into the clay pots, he explains. The saliva enzymes ferment the liquid. I grimace. It is the first time I hear Angel laugh.

*

We take a long boat ride and hike to see the Yagua Indians. The elders don the traditional grass skirts for visitors, sell amulets and bowls and belts. Children swarm around a tourist who hands out rubber bands. Tiny hands pull at the bag and yellow, red, green and blue rubber bands spray all over the ground. The children scramble like pigeons in a park. I search my pack for something to offer. Cough drops and a Wash 'n Dry are all I have. Someone gives them gum and they throw the wrappers on the ground. The ladies in the group cluck, and instruct the children to pick up the papers. Roldan talks with the Indians, jokes around with a blow gun. I look for Angel. He is leaning against a tree on the edge of the opening, watching.

"It's a shame," one woman says about him. "He's an intelligent man."

"So good looking too," another says. Even the older, married women with their retired doctor and businessman husbands fantasise. One woman is paying Angel an extra $20 to take her to hunt for tarantulas. The other women ask to come, and Angel leads five of us into the jungle. He stops, tells us to cut our lights, be still.

"Listen," he says. We stand in complete blackness. He scans his flashlight across the path, finds a hole in the ground and shoves a stick into it. A tarantula comes crawling out, furry and fat, like a pet.

"Touch it," he says, but we are afraid of its bite.

*

For the remaining nights Angel and I meet. On the last night, sheets of rain pour down on the palm thatch roof over our heads like bullets. I feel warm air from his nose on my throat. Outside the rain stops, and the insects and owls and night creatures call with urgency.

At the airport, Angel hugs me. I leave him my money, my flashlight, my day pack, not much, but things he can use. I put my address and phone number in the pack. On the plane I stare out the window, the sharp peaks of the Andes like knives that could cut into the silver belly of our plane. I dream that I return home pregnant, don't tell anyone, just let the life grow inside me, and then push and pull into this world a half-wild child. Tiny, brown, a swimmer, a small fish in a wide river, a dolphin child, a piranha like his father.

from
One Room in a Castle

Karen Connelly

Karen Connelly is a native of Calgary, Canada, and has lived in Thailand, Spain and France. Now resident in Greece, she is the author of *One Room in a Castle*, *Touch the Dragon* and three poetry collections, *The Small Words in My Body*, *This Brighter Prison* and *The Disorder of Love*.

La Poésie dans un Jardin

The sign says *Librairie et Centre des Rencontres*. Poetry books are displayed in the window; I go inside. How civilised, I think, a bookstore and a meeting place for Avignonnaise writers and artists. A large storefront room with high ceilings, La Poésie dans un Jardin is lined with bookshelves, scattered with mismatched tables, ashtrays, papers. Water stains darken the ceiling and cracks spider over the walls. A sign hanging on the hook of a small door reads 'The toilet is out of order'. Beneath it, someone has scribbled *again* in a different hand. I am, I think, the only customer in the store.

At the far end of the long room, two men and a woman sit around a card table, arguing vehemently. I crane my neck. James Joyce. They are arguing about James Joyce. A pile of books sits on the table. They talk at the same time, almost yelling, gesticulating in the precise, indignant way of the French, rolling their eyes, pouting their lips. The French always seem so astonished, so indignant that other people's opinions differ from their own. As the woman's cheeks flush with exertion, her eyes get bluer, her opinion louder. Curvaceously plump, strong-looking, she speaks with a cigarette voice. The two men are opposites. One is small and chubby, pale, with a bald spot pinking through his dark, almost greasy hair. He reminds me of uncooked pastry. The other man is a tall, thin, coffee-skinned Arab, with a wiry mess of black and grey-streaked hair pulled away from his face.

The Arab's voice is deep as a subterranean cave. The most indignant of all, he makes his own echoes. His black eyes spark and widen with outrage. He wears a long black scarf, the end of which he sometimes lashes against the table top for emphasis. I can't understand what he says, but he looks great. I haven't been here long enough to eavesdrop on passionate, three-way arguments, but I do the best I can, navigating closer one bookshelf at a time. I am dizzy by the time the pale man puts his hands in his corduroy lap and interrupts in a quiet voice, "Wait, wait. Are we going to have a coffee or not? I had the impression we came in here for a coffee."

The woman immediately gets up from the small card table. "But yes, of course, Arthur, I completely forgot." She disappears behind a curtain. The Arabic man asks after her, "Do you have anything to drink?" Arthur looks at me inquisitively for the third or fourth time. I stand in front of the closest bookshelf, holding a poetry collection by René Char. When the pale man speaks again, I have my back to him, but I know he's talking to me. "Would you like a coffee, too?"

I turn around, smiling. How much gratitude shows on my face?

Too much. Entirely too much.

Show me something beautiful
After the coffee, Shaquil, the Arab, leans toward me and asks, "Do you think we should, ahh, go for a walk through the streets of Avignon?"

I am here, as easily, as miraculously as breathing in. I could be anywhere else on earth but I am here, and now I have found three people, we are speaking, I am no longer alone. A man with pitch-black eyes leans forward (I can smell cigarettes and sweat, his African skin) and asks me to go for a walk with him. I stand up and thank Marie for the coffee and shake Arthur's deboned white hand. Wind hammers at the windows. Shaquil holds the door open as I button up my coat and wrap a scarf around my head.

A walk through Avignon like a waltz, with the streetlights flickering on and the wind in our throats as we speak. I stumble over French and flagstones. Shaquil walks too quickly, which I like, because we're half-running, warm, breathless, pulling each other up the palace stairs and around the tight street corners. The squares and courtyards are empty, but warm yellow light reaches out from restaurant windows.

The labyrinth of streets around the palace have names like songs and we sing ourselves through them. From Rue Banasterie to Rue des Trois Colombes, onto Carnot, past the flower shop, around again, almost in a circle, to Rue Ste Catherine. Rue Peyrollerie. Roll the syllables from the throat, and remember this: the Street of the Three Falcons. Shaquil takes me to see the famous carved door of a cathedral and shows me the shop of ancient books. "They had a 300-year-old Bible once, and an even older Koran two years ago. You wouldn't believe how rich some of the people around here are. This house, see the crossbeams, the narrow doors, those windows. It was built in the sixteenth century. Full of antiques. One curtain cost more than my car. No! I've never been inside but I used to go out with one of the maids. C'est vrai. She used to steal wine for me." The great clanging palace bells strike the hour, but I lose count. Is it nine or ten? Or eleven?

The later it gets, the hungrier and happier I become. Light-headed, laughing, I say, "I feel drunk."

Shaquil hits me lightly with his scarf. "That's because you're breathing more than your share of the air. Leave some for me! I'm an old man." I look at him from the corner of my eye. Thirty-five? With a lot of grey and white hair. We stop walking at the same time and stand in the unlit street. I hold my breath. On either side are very tall, old houses. The highest window of one of them is unshuttered. A woman in the attic is singing. "What language is that?"

"Polish?"

"Hungarian?"

We listen for a couple of minutes, our hearts beating slow. Our heads lean far back. We wish she would appear at the window. She doesn't. We walk on.

So I enter Avignon with a raven of a man whose loose black coat sleeves flap as he talks. His hands fly up to point out gargoyles and stone reliefs above doorways. We walk around the back of the palace, where one of its unfinished rock walls rises like the face of a mountain. Opposite, on the wall of another building, painted figures loom out of painted windows. They are eerily out of place, these jovial men and women grinning at the palace, at each other. "It's for the festival, the summer theatre festival, the only time this place isn't a graveyard. You're staying until the summer, aren't you? Then you'll understand why anyone lives here. It becomes a French Venice during the summer, full of foreigners and artists and acrobats."

We walk back into the maze of streets. In a square I don't recognise, Shaquil tells me to close my eyes.

"Why?"

"What kind of a question is that, why? Because I want to surprise you." We stop walking and turn to each other. He makes a face. "Don't you trust me?"

"Yes, but why do you want me to close my eyes?" Closing my eyes in Avignon strikes me as a dangerous act.

"Merde, c'est incroyable. Tu es vraiment dure. Une dure canadienne."

"This has nothing to do with being Canadian, Shaquil."

"You don't trust me?"

"I don't know."

"Merde, don't be so serious. I want to show you something beautiful. Let me blindfold you." He unwraps the long black scarf from around his neck.

A couple walks by us just now, past a darkened storefront. Both the woman and the man shoot me a disapproving look. Not a concerned look, not a look that says, "You silly foreign girl, don't you realise this is the town rapist?" No, their expressions bother me because they so easily and quickly convey disgust. Disgust and anger. They don't look at Shaquil, only at me.

I am confused. Shaquil swears under his breath, but I don't understand. "What is it?"

"Ma piel," he says in an angry voice, then, in the next moment, smiles broadly and flicks the end of his black scarf toward the couple, who is already far down the street. "Votre problème."

When I see his face now, after seeing theirs, I remember. He is Algerian, a very dark Algerian. And I am quite white, especially in the dark. The contrast is the source of their disgust and their anger. The clarity of this delayed realisation makes me furious. They don't approve of the mixture here, they don't like it. The colour combination offends their fashion sensibilities: we don't *match*.

"All right," I return Shaquil's smile and open my arms. "Blindfold me. Show me something beautiful."

He wraps the scarf around my eyes twice, enveloping me in darkness. The scarf smells like Shaquil: sweat, cigarettes, skin, cold night air, something vaguely minty. And then the smell of the street, settled car exhaust, night-dampened stone . . . paint? Could someone have been painting here today? My feet consciously remember what I've already come to take for granted: the treacherous nature of cobblestones. I smell the faint but growing scent of food. He walks me forward, down, up – it can't be very far but it feels far because I'm blind, half-floating, unsure of where the ground is, convinced we are walking past trees and one of the lower branches will hit me. Now I feel buildings rise up on either side. The wind doesn't blow here. The sound of his voice has a new solidity to it.

I hold Shaquil's arm, but not too tightly. Once over the initial lack of balance and the weird shiftiness of the unseen world, I enjoy the intense blend of fear and excitement. Braid upon braid of delicious scents loosen in the air as we move forward. My mouth waters. What food is this? A steamed smell like rice, but it's not rice, is it? The smell of vegetables, some tender meat turned and simmered in a garden of spices, herbs, seasonings I don't recognise, except by colour: ochre and saffron, burgundy, heavy crimson, olive-oiled gold.

"Now we have to go up –" we step up a curb "– and down. Another one. One more." I'm sniffing the air. Shaquil laughs. "Comme un chien. T'as faim, eh? Moi aussi. Now just stand there a moment while I open the door. Because it's heavy."

"Can I take off the blindfold?"

"Absolument pas!"

When he opens the door, I hear music for the first time. Indian music? North African? Cretan? After passing through one door, then another, we are inside both the music and the intoxicating smell of the food, buoyed on a quiet sea of human voices.

"I'm taking off the blindfold now, I can't stand it any more."

"Wait. I'll do it." He stands behind me and undoes the unwieldy woollen knot. Unwrap, unwrap –

– and I open my eyes, squinting, dazzled. Where are we? In

a tent in Morocco. In the Algerian desert. In a Bedouin camp on the edge of an oasis. Rugs hang above and spread below us, fabrics woven with gold and bronze threads, low tables and embroidered cushions crowd the shadowed corners. Oil lamps burn on the walls. Men in long gowns carry platters of fragrant food past us. One of them greets Shaquil, hugs him, and grins at me in a greasy, sexual way. (Am I the twelfth foreign woman that Shaquil has blindfolded and brought here? Have I just played a part in the theatre of Shaquil?) The grinner and Shaquil speak Arabic together for a couple of minutes, then the grinner leads us to a table inlaid with silver. We take off our shoes before we sit down on the cushions. One of the men – who are so solemnly graceful that I hesitate to call them waiters – places an ornate silver bowl beneath our hands, then pours warm water over them.

"Now," Shaquil says, "our hands are clean. We are going to eat a feast."

The south of France
(or, A tiny piece of the big yes)

Harira soup. Charred and peeled peppers garnished with fresh green cilantro. *B'stilla* of cinnamon and ginger. The most expensive Medoc on the menu. Fine gold phyllo stuffed with shrimp. The aroma of paprika and fresh flat bread. More Medoc. Phyllo stuffed with spinach. Lemon wedges and a blue bowl of Moroccan olives. Medoc once more. Sole tagine with the spicy *elhout m'chermel*. Lamb couscous. The last of the second bottle of Medoc. Mint tea, poured from a silver pot and an impressive height. Strawberries and almonds, soaked in sweet syrup.

But no sex.

He is very civil about it. "Je veux pas le grand Oui tout entier," he explains to me in his car, an expression of persuasive logic on his face. "Je veux seulment un petit morceau de le grand Oui." I don't want the entire big Yes. I just want a tiny piece of it.

I cough. "I have to go in. It's late."

"Dure. Une dure canadienne."

"Oui, c'est moi. Comme la pierre." I knock my forehead with my knuckles.

He looks out the window at the looming concrete apartment blocks of my neighbourhood. "You really live here? This is the worst part of Montclar. Even I wouldn't walk here alone at night."

"Yes, I really live here. It's not so bad."

"Do you carry a knife?"

"Are you kidding? Of course not."

After saying goodnight, I leap out of the car before he can give me more than a grasping embrace. When I reach the door of my building, he blows me a kiss and drives away.

But the building isn't mine.

The building looks just like mine – a prison block – but the number is different. I walk to the next concrete barricade, turning my face away from the icy wind. None of those buildings is mine, either. Shaquil's car is long gone, though I walk out of the complex of apartment buildings and peer down the road, praying he will be persistent in his desire for a tiny piece of the big yes.

But he doesn't come back.

Across the street, I see a long row of scorched, windowless buildings, a heap of bricks and refuse in a vacant lot, a burned-out car half a block down the road. Do you carry a knife?

I haven't the faintest idea where I am. When Shaquil drove me here, it all looked vaguely familiar, in a drowsy, drunken sort of way. In Avignon, I never ride in cars; streets seen from inside a car always look slightly different.

All right. If I don't know where I am, I must at least pretend that I know where I am. Turning in circles and wandering from one building to the next is sure to attract thieves and assassins. As I walk up the street I think we drove down to get here, my teeth start chattering. I pull my collar up around my ears, push my hands deep into my coat pockets, clench my teeth but the chatter seems to travel into my shoulders, shaking them as I walk. Whenever I see a man walking toward me, I turn down a side street to avoid passing him. This brings utter disorientation and a profound sense of doom. I can't ask any of those men for directions because if I speak, they'll hear my accent, and all those warped synapses in their brains will connect and spark like lightning. What's a nice foreign girl like you doing in a ghetto like this at three in the morning?

The wind demon-howls down the street. My feet are as cold as the concrete beneath them. But it's the cold that keeps me safe; few people venture out in such icy wind.

Wait. Could it be? There, in the distance, is my little *boulangerie*. And farther down the street is the corner of the old house with the ceramic snail on the roof. I am, by some miracle or merciful accident, finding my way home. I am too tired to run to the entrance way, but there it is, my own complex of ugly apartment buildings. Lucette and 200 pigeons are sleeping up there, on the third floor. I'm so happy I want to hug the entire building, but instead I find my keys and fumble at the lock with stiff fingers.

Beautiful island

"Winter in Provence always makes me sad," Isabelle sighs. She smiles and looks down into her espresso cup. "It's much nicer in

Paris. Greyer, yes, but warmer. More friendly." In Isabelle's very small, white hands, an espresso cup almost seems like a normal size. "The mistral makes my varicose veins get worse." She stretches her leg out from the table and squints down at her black-sheathed calves. "Merde! Just like worms! I only have a couple, but they are the ugliest things . . ." We are sitting in the dubiously named Bar Americain, on Avignon's main street.

When I tell her about my misadventure in Montclar a few nights ago, she immediately says, "But Shaquil should have known better than to drop you off in the Arab quartier! Stupid man."

"You know him?"

"Of course I know him. He owes me money. He owes everyone money. Has he asked to borrow from you yet?"

"Uh, no."

"Ha! But you only met him a few days ago, isn't that true?"

When I don't reply, she raises one thin eyebrow. "What? What's this? You don't *like* him, do you?" When I say nothing, she starts to choke. The red-nailed fingers clutch at her throat.

"We only had supper together."

"I hope! But supper can lead to death. Any Catholic knows that. Shaquil is crazy."

"I think he's beautiful."

"And I *know* he is crazy. Brilliant but cracked." With her small hands she expertly mimes cracking an egg on the edge of the café table. Then she laughs. "Don't give me such a disapproving look. I won't say another word . . . well, maybe just one or two. But you will see. Just wait. Lucky girl." She tosses the invisible eggshells over her shoulders.

Isabelle! Her name means 'beautiful island'. She was raised in a *banlieue* of Paris, and worked in the city until she was twenty-four, but to me she is pure Avignon. I asked her out for coffee after a movie because she was the only other woman there alone, and the only other one who laughed at the funny parts.

Isabelle is a prostitute. She's the happiest person I know here. Not to say she is always happy. "The tragedy of cold weather is that we are all obliged to wear too many clothes." Every time I see her, she is wearing black lace-up boots with wedge heels. "Winter apparel," she explains. Boots of the latest fashion or boots that are eighty years old? Impossible to tell with Isabelle. She also wears a black mohair coat that hugs her waist and drops smoothly off her hips; a garment from another age, especially when combined with her little black pillbox hat. She commands the eye, above all the first time you see her, across the street or coming out of a shop, when you don't know the softer angles of her face. There is nothing coarse or cheap about Isabelle; don't imagine her the wrong way. She is like a blonde movie star (elegant French, not brash American) on the rain-slick street, her black outfit striking against the white stones of the museum. She coils her hair up on her head like a gold rope, lets it go wispy at the back of her neck and around her oval face. A very young, beautiful woman's face (though she is no longer very young), with a small, full mouth. She always wears the same shade of red lipstick. (She applies it, leaves it on for a few seconds, then wipes most of it off, leaving only the dye on her lips. When I asked her why she did this, she glared at me, pretending to be insulted. "What do you think I am? Eh? A whore?" We laughed until we couldn't breathe.)

When she walks by, we hear the *clickclack clickclack* of her boots around the puddles. *Clickclack clickclack*, then a pause when she stops at the shop windows, as she often does, because she loves clothes. Black fishnet stockings are high fashion this year, a fact that amuses her. "They'll never lose their power to seduce," she said. "Traditional putain attire secretly appeals to everyone. Fishnet stockings, for example." She shimmied her shoulders. "And now housewives and economics students are wearing them. Bravo! Who said progress was an illusion?"

One afternoon Marie, from La Poésie dans un Jardin, watched her pass in front of the window and whispered to me, "Bizarre that one of the most beautiful women in Provence chooses to sell her beauty."

I am beginning to wonder if it is bizarre.

Isabelle, after all, has a sharp sense of humour laced with humane irony, excellent business savvy, and good tables in all the best restaurants of Avignon and Aix-en-Provence. Once, I ventured to ask her if she was happy.

Vaguely surprised, she answered me with her own question, "Wouldn't you be?"

When we go for coffee, she rarely talks about her work. She talks about the latest 'release' of wine like a publisher talks about new books. Isabelle studies wines for a hobby; she has an entire oak bookshelf devoted to the wine-making regions of France, Italy, Portugal and Spain. She talks about her brother who lives in Montpellier, and his daughter, who recently turned four years old and has started cello lessons. She talks about the new CDs she's bought, and makes me listen numerous times to her favourite songs or classical pieces.

Today she keeps sliding back to the topic of Shaquil. "He told you how he grew up in Algeria?"

"A little." I try to sound uninterested.

"His father was a double agent for the Algerian and French governments."

"A spy? Really?"

"Yes. It's quite true. The family was often in danger. Shaquil will tell you when he gets drunk. Those are his worst and best memories: the whole family terrified, crossing the desert with a single flashlight and the clothes on their backs."

"When did he come to France?"

"As a young man, for university. How many of them came here when Algeria was still under French rule! After learning our language in Africa and loving our literature and believing that they were more French than Algerian. Shaquil studied at the Sorbonne. He has memorised more French poetry than I have ever read. But still this country is not his home."

"But why do you say he is crazy?"

"After university, he married a Parisienne, someone he had studied with. They had two children. When they came to Avignon –"

"Why did they come here?"

"Because Shaquil was offered a job teaching Arabic literature at the university. But his wife was never happy here. Who knows? Maybe she was never happy in Paris, either. These are secrets." The *peck-peck-peck* rhythm of gossip is gone from Isabelle's voice. Stretching her leg out from under the table again, she plucks a long blonde hair from the black gauze of her nylons. "She committed suicide. Four, maybe five years ago. With the children in the apartment next door. Shaquil has never been the same. Last year, her parents took him to court and won custody of the children. He was unfit to be a father, they said." She puts one leg over the other and slides them back under the table. "Probably they were right. Poor bastard."

Othello

There he is. Shaquil the Arab, walking down Rue de la

République like a king, his white teeth gleaming like gems in his head, and his eyes, black gems. You would fall in love with him, too, if you could see him. Shakespeare knew something about the tantalising bones of the Arab face. Othellos are everywhere in France, the handsomest, loneliest men on earth. Shaquil flips his black scarf around his neck, smiles at his own reflection, tips his hat to small, tight-mouthed white ladies. A rose between his teeth would not be out of place. In fact, I have seen him with a rose between his teeth more than once. The black hat is set at a jaunty angle, like his shoulders, like the line of his right eyebrow. You can see the thick strands of white in his hair, the perfect cut of his trousers. In the pockets of the long black coat, you will find a twig of pine, some green, sharp-scented sprig. He gives me a small pine branch every time he comes to meet me.

In a kitchen full of dried herbs covered with dust, he made mint tea in a silver pot. "This taste is the desert where I was born." He recited Baudelaire and St John Perse. He's painted poetry in classical Arabic calligraphy on the white and blue walls of his apartment. After lighting the candles on the table, on the book-shelves, on the thickly carpeted floor, Shaquil read the walls to me.

After the first bottle of wine, he began to talk quietly. I leaned closer to hear him. He whispered because he was telling secrets. Every one of his secrets became a question. What happened to his wife? Where are his children now? How to make sense of two empty hands? His eyes were very black. I smelled wax and all the cigarettes he'd smoked since his thirteenth year. He seemed to be trembling.

I was afraid of the immediate closeness, the rockslide of words. I was afraid that if we embraced, we would knock over a candle and set the apartment on fire. He had conspired to get me into his apartment to achieve a smooth seduction. But instead, he moved, without lust, into my arms, where he began to cry.

He moulded his bony length into my arms, my stomach, my hips, my legs. I held his angular shoulders and his head of thick hair. The candles burned down as he wept.

Single portions

I walk from Armelle's house to the post office thinking of Pablo Neruda, who said that the literature of Europe exists in its rooms, never outside, under the real sky. But it's more than the literature. Armelle lives her life in two tiny, joined rooms. I think of all the people I know in this town who reside in strange, cramped little apartments, attic flats with sloped roofs, the back bedrooms of family houses, rented, makeshift lodgings. Rooms inhabited by cats – always, always by cats – and dust and an overwhelming atmosphere of decay, of aging, of loss. To ward off emptiness, the people who live in these spaces fill, clutter and pack them to bursting, until freedom to move is the only thing they don't have. Cats, old books, an empty fish tank, shelves crammed with 5000 accumulated objects, two dozen pilfered espresso cups, antique tables, a guitar no one can play. And draped over it all like another old silk scarf, the smell of cloying perfume, cat piss, the faint reek of a strong cheese.

Above the sink of dirty coffee cups and saucers, a narrow shelf is lined with single-portion cans of peas and tuna. Ah, Mediterranean fare. So many people, like Armelle, like myself, open these little cans, empty them into bowls of silence, and eat alone. In this apartment, the step from eating alone to dying alone looks very small indeed.

Armelle's cat has had another litter of kittens. Her fridge is broken, but milk in a bottle still sits inside, turning green. She says she has no time to clean up the other room in the apartment, though it's a grand, high-ceilinged chamber with French windows. (French windows. Of course. Every window in this country is French.) This excellent room is piled high, crammed full of her ex-husband's boxes. Ugh! Her ex-husband, who left her six years ago for another woman. And she still lets him have the most beautiful room in her house!

Friday. An impossible day. Depressing morning coffee at Armelle's. For breakfast, she fed me a distant relative of porridge; it tasted of stable dust. I imagine I have the rancid perfume of cat piss on my skin. Cat hair clings to my black trousers. Stupid clothes! I want to cash a cheque today and buy a skirt. Damn. The post office has closed early. What do you mean the post office has closed early? I can't mail my bushel of letters. The chain of words in my universe now dangles in space, touching nothing. The shops are packed full of elbows and obnoxious clerks. I back out of the shops. I take my cheque to the bank.

Unfortunately, it's not quite as international as I hoped. The sharp-nosed clerk glances up at me from behind her large glasses. A tight little voice escapes her lips, "I can't cash this."

"Are you sure? They told me it was international."

Bank clerk snorts her annoyance, "C'est impossible."

Slight desperation sets in. "Could you please talk to the supervisor about it?"

Turning on heel, the bank clerk hammers away in her heavy shoes. She returns triumphant, a malicious grin on her face. "I was right. It is impossible to cash this cheque."

Fine, fine, maybe she's being a bitch because she hates my black trousers. Everyone does. Even I do.

Hoping to salvage something from this ruined transaction, I

attempt humour. I raise my eyebrows and say, "I guess I'll starve to death this month." She doesn't even smile.

I leave the bank dejected. Then I remember: Marie has said on numerous occasions that she would lend me money if I ever had banking problems. I begin to think, All will be well, when I see a bad omen striding toward me. A murderer. Obviously a murderer, that man, why isn't he carrying an axe? He's one of those lean, muscular men with colourless hair that can't remember being washed, a jean jacket whose sleeves are too short, gnawed-looking wrists, arms that do not swing but hang down by his sides (the hands grip invisible blunt objects). Blue, staring eyes betray a savage interior landscape. Wild boars live in that man's skull.

But who knows, really? He's probably nicer than the bank clerk. He mutters something at me as we pass each other, but I can't decipher it.

I decide not to go to the park beside the palace. I start walking back down Rue de la République. No energy. There will be lonely men in the park, there always are. Lonely men who stare and stare, at the women, at the girls, at the little girls who feed the swans. Too depressing. Thieves and assassins. And bank clerks. And rooms full of cats. Letters I cannot send. Money I cannot get.

On my way home, when I pass the house that has a ceramic snail on its roof, I start to cry. That snail! What a joke. The concrete makes me cry; there is so much of it. There is no grass. Did I tell you, spring is coming? It's never winter forever, but do you know what the people here do? They build walls around their gardens. And if they can't build walls, they erect chainlink fences, then cover the fences in netting. No one out in the street can see inside. The people hide their gardens.

I take it personally. It seems as if they have walls simply to prevent me from being close to the earth, close to colour, close to growing things. But I manage it anyway. I peer through the chinks and crevices and unintentional openings. No one can keep me from the vision of spring inside. Trees are budding now. Even the little vegetable plots are spiked with shoots. Lilac bushes, flowers I can't name, plants, ivy greening on the walls, slow unfurling of leaves.

I howl walking home, inconsolable, defeated by fences. Cloistered gardens. Earth suffocating beneath cement.

Liaison dangereuse

"You made love with me once, and now you're telling me you won't make love with me again?"

Pause of embarrassed hesitation. "Yes." Shaquil and I are sitting in his car. My fingers rest on the door handle.

"Then why did you sleep with me in the first place?"

Just how stupid will my reason sound? "Because I thought it would help you." Oh, God, *very* stupid.

"You slept with me out of pity?"

"No, of course not."

"Then why won't you sleep with me again?"

"Can we talk about this when we haven't drunk so much wine?"

"No! Moi, je comprends rien. Dis-moi. Qu'est-ce que tu me fais?" He bangs the steering wheel with his fist and the whole apparatus rattles. His face is so altered in anger that I would not recognise him if I passed him on the street. He has become ugly.

"I don't *want* to come home with you."

His lips curl up, revealing purplish gums and tobacco-stained teeth. He is snarling at me. "J'ai peur de toi," I tell him.

"You're afraid of me! I'm the one who should be afraid of you, crazy woman, for fucking with my head." As the swearing picks up momentum, I really do feel afraid. I don't even understand some of the things he calls me, but he is screaming. A violent word is a violent act. I push open the car door and almost fall into the street, so anxious am I to get out. He reaches for me as I scramble away. He would pull me back in if he could, but I'm out now, walking quickly toward my beloved prison block. I ignore Shaquil's shouts. He remains in his car but through the open window he continues yelling questions and obscenities.

I open the door, press the timer-light, run up the four flights of stairs to my door. His voice is just barely audible from here; the apartment is on the far side of the building, away from the street. Lucette says hello. She sticks her head out the kitchen door. "What's wrong with you?"

I hang up my sweater to gain a moment's respite from the inevitable questions. Then, mumbling something about being tired, I take off my shoes. But Lucette can see fear in my face, in the movements of my arms and legs. She can probably smell fear. "What happened to you?"

"Ce n'est pas grave. I just had an argument with Shaquil."

"Ah, he's a bad type, that one. You won't see him again, eh?"

"No. No, I don't think I'll see him again."

"Better for you. These Arabs, they're so –"

"Lucette, it has nothing to do with him being an Arab –"

We are interrupted by an unmistakable voice. Four floors below. Beneath my bedroom window. "Karenne! Karenne! C'est pas juste, ce que tu me fais maintenant. Tu es trop pragmatique! Tu es froide parce que tu viens de Canada!"

"Mon Dieu," says Lucette, clutching the collar of her blouse together, as if Shaquil's voice alone has the power to rip off her

115

clothes. "Il est fou. I will call the police! They will come and take him away, filthy man."

"Lucette, there's no need to call the police. I'll just . . ." What? What will I do? "I'll just go into my bedroom and talk to him."

"You'll talk to him from your bedroom window? We're four floors up!"

"I don't want to go down."

"But all the neighbours . . ."

"The neighbours will enjoy it, Lucette. It's better than television."

I open up my long French windows and lean over the small balcony. "Shaquil!"

"Tu es froide et dure."

"Oui, t'as raison. I am cold and hard. Thank you. No one has ever told me that before."

"What? I can't hear you."

I repeat myself in a louder voice.

"It's not a compliment!" He swears at me. Again. And some more. Lights go on in the adjacent apartment. Lucette stands behind me, at my bedroom door, summoning God and the Holy Mother. I am suddenly overwhelmed by a desire to laugh. It is all I can do to keep from howling with laughter as Shaquil calls me a bitch, a cunt, a liar.

None of this is funny. But it's so melodramatic. And the neighbours really are listening. Curtains across the street open slightly, like squinting eyes. An old woman's face peers out. Melodrama embarrasses me. When I am embarrassed, I usually laugh. There is nothing amusing about Shaquil's violent tendencies and his fierce struggle with himself and the world. But this, the balcony soap-opera rendition, the stupidity of it, my own and his, the gorgeous angry man in a hat standing below my window, yelling my name, pissing off my hard-faced neighbours, *this* is funny, in a pitiable, wearing sort of way. Like a Woody Allen movie interrupted by Fellini, or the other way around.

We shout back and forth for a while. Shaquil's neck must be getting sore from looking up. Finally, Lucette comes to the balcony and, raising a fist, yells threats about the police. An outraged Provençal accent is truly frightening: Shaquil leaves. I apologise to Lucette, profusely, and promise that it will never happen again. "This is your own fault, Karenne. I told you before I even met him that he was a bad type. Zoot! Madame Farnoux, across the way, will talk about this for two months. Drunken Arabs! No more! It will be the last time this happens or you will find yourself another place to live!"

I take a shower. Then I make myself a cup of tea and collapse into bed. I feel like I've just done an intensive course at a famous university. 'Liaisons Dangereuses 406', or 'La Deconstruction d'Alcoolisme 302', or 'Les Politiques Sexuelles 601'. Or all of them in the same semester, while reading Sartre's translation of *Wuthering Heights*.

Sweating Profusely in Mérida: A Memoir

Carol Queen

Carol Queen is a writer and cultural sexologist whose journey towards a PhD (frequently interrupted by diversions like trips to Mérida) is almost complete. Soon she'll do more than 'play' doctor. She is the author of *Real Live Nude Girl: Chronicles of Sex-Positive Culture* (Cleis) and *Exhibitionism for the Shy* (Down There Press).

The Boyfriend and I met at a sex party. I was in a back room trying to help facilitate an erection for a gentleman brought to the party by a woman who would have nothing to do with him once they got there. She had charged him a pretty penny to get in, and I actually felt that I should have gotten every cent, but I suppose it was my own fault that I was playing Mother Teresa and didn't know when to let go of the man's dick. Boyfriend was hiding behind a potted palm eyeing me and this guy's uncooperative, uncut dick, and it seemed Boyfriend had a thing for pretty girls *and* uncut men, especially the latter. So he decided to help me out and replaced my hand with his mouth. That was when it got interesting. The uncut straight guy finally left and I stayed.

In the few months our relationship lasted, we shared many more straight men, most of them – Boyfriend's radar was incredible – uncircumcised and willing to do almost anything with a man as long as there was a woman in the room. I often acted as sort of a hook to hang a guy's heterosexuality on while Boyfriend sucked his dick or even fucked him. My favourite was the hitchhiker wearing pink lace panties under his grungy jeans – but that's another story. Long before we met him, Boyfriend had invited me to go to Mexico.

This was the plan. Almost all the guys in Mexico are uncut, right? And lots will play with men, too, Boyfriend assured me, especially if there's a woman there. (I guessed they resembled American men in this respect.) Besides, it would be a romantic vacation.

That was how we wound up in Room 201 of the Hotel

Reforma in sleepy Mérida, capital of the Yucatán. Mérida's popularity as a tourist town had been eclipsed by the growth of Cancún, the nearest Americanised resort. That meant the boys would be hornier, Boyfriend reasoned. The Hotel Reforma had been recommended by a fellow foreskin fancier. Its chief advantages were the price – about $14 a night – and the fact that the management didn't charge extra for extra guests. I liked it because it was old, airy and cool, with wrought-iron railings and floor tiles worn thin from all the people who'd come before. Boyfriend liked it because it had a pool, always a good place to cruise, and a disco across the street. That's where we headed as soon as we got in from the airport, showered, and changed into skimpy clothes suitable for turning tropical boys' heads.

There were hardly any tropical boys there, as it turned out, because this was where the Ft Lauderdale college students who couldn't afford spring break in Cancún went to spend their more meagre allowances, and not only did it look like a Mexican restaurant-with-disco in Ft Lauderdale, the management took care to keep all but the most dapper Méridans out lest the coeds be frightened by scruffy street boys. Scruffy street boys, of course, is just what Boyfriend had his eye out for, and at first the pickings looked slim; but we found one who had slipped past security, out to hustle nothing more spicy than a gig showing tourists around the warren of narrow streets near the town's central plaza, stumbling instead onto us. Ten minutes later Boyfriend had his mouth wrapped around a meaty little bundle, *with* foreskin. Luis stuck close to us for several days, probably eating more regularly than usual, and wondering out loud whether all the women in America were like me, and would we take him back with us? Or at least send him a Motley Crüe T-shirt when we went home?

Boyfriend had brought Bob Damron's gay travel guide, which listed for Mérida: a cruisy restaurant (it wasn't) and a cruisy park bench in the Zocalo (it was, and one night Boyfriend stayed out most of the night looking for gay men, who, he said, would run the other way if they saw me coming, and found one, a slender boy who had to pull down the panty hose he wore under his jeans so Boyfriend could get to his cock, and who expressed wonder because he had never seen anyone with so many condoms; in fact most people never had condoms at all. Boyfriend gave him his night's supply and some little brochures about *el SIDA* he'd brought from the AIDS Foundation, *en español* so even if our limited Spanish didn't get through to our tricks, a pamphlet might).

Damron's also indicated that Mérida had a bathhouse.

I had always wanted to go to a bathhouse, and of course there was not much chance it would ever happen back home. For one thing, they were all closed before I ever moved to San Francisco. For another, even if I dressed enough like a boy to pass, I wouldn't look old enough to be let in. But in Mérida perhaps things were different.

It was away from the town's centre, but within walking distance of the Hotel Reforma. Through the tiny front window, grimy from the town's blowing dust, I saw a huge papier-mâché figure of Pan, painted brightly and hung with jewellery, phallus high. It looked like something the Radical Faeries would carry in the Gay Day parade. Everything else about the lobby looked dingy, like the waiting room of a used-car dealership.

Los Baños de Vapor would open at eight that evening. They had a central tub and rooms to rent; massage boys could be rented, too. I would be welcome.

The papier-mâché Pan was at least seven feet tall and was

indeed the only bright thing in the lobby. Passing through the courtyard, an overgrown jumble of vines pushing through cracked tile, a slight smell of sulphur, a stagnant fountain, we were shown up a flight of concrete stairs to our room by Carlos, a solid, round-faced man in his mid-twenties, wrapped in a frayed white towel. The room was small and completely tiled, grout black from a losing fight with the wet tropical air. At one end was a shower and at the other a bench, a low, vinyl-covered bed, and a massage table. There was a switch that, when flipped, filled the room with steam. Boyfriend flipped it and we shucked our clothes; as the pipes hissed and clanked, Carlos gestured to the massage table and then to me.

Boyfriend answered for me, in Spanish, that I'd love to. I got on the table and Carlos set to work. Boyfriend danced around the table gleefully, sometimes stroking me, sometimes Carlos's butt. "Hey, man, I'm working!" Carlos protested, not very insistently, and Boyfriend went for his cock, stroking it hard, then urged him up onto the table, and Carlos's hands, still slick from the massage oil and warm from the friction of my skin, covered my breasts as Boyfriend rolled a condom onto Carlos's cock and rubbed it up and down my labia a few times and finally let go, letting it sink in. He rode me slow and then hard while the table rocked dangerously and Boyfriend stood at my head, letting me tongue his cock while he played with Carlos's tits. When Boyfriend was sure that we were having a good time, he put on a towel and slipped out the door. Carlos looked surprised. I had to figure out how to say, in Spanish, "He's going hunting," and get him to go back to fucking me, solid body slick from oil and steam; if he kept it up, he would make me come, clutching his slippery back, legs in the air.

That was just happening when Boyfriend came back with

David. He was pulling him in the door by his already stiff penis, and I suspected Boyfriend had wasted as little time getting him by the dick as he usually did. He had found David in the tub room, he announced, and he had a beautiful, long *uncut* cock. (Boyfriend always enunciated clearly when he said "uncut.") David *did* have a beautiful cock, and he spoke English and was long and slim with startling blue eyes. It turned out he was Chicano, second generation, a senior at Riverside High who spent school breaks with his grandmother in Mérida and worked at Los Baños de Vapor as a secret summer job. We found out all this about him as I was showering the sweat and oil off from my fuck with Carlos, and by the time I heard that he'd been working at the Baños since he turned sixteen, I was ready to start fucking again. David was the most quintessentially eighteen-year-old fuck I ever had, except Boyfriend's presence made it unusual; he held David's cock and balls and controlled the speed of the thrusting, until his mouth got preoccupied with Carlos's dick. David told me, ardently, that I was beautiful, though at that point I didn't care if I was beautiful or not, since I was finally in a bathhouse doing what I'd always wanted to do and I felt more like a faggot than a beautiful *gringa*. But David was saying he wished he had a girlfriend like me, even though I was thirty, shockingly old – this actually was what almost all of Boyfriend's conquests said to me, though I suspected not every man could keep up with a girlfriend who was really a faggot, or a boyfriend who was really a woman, or whatever kind of fabulous anomaly I was.

Then someone knocked on the door and we untangled for a minute to answer it, and there were José and Gaspar, laughing and saying we were the most popular room in the Baños at the moment and would we like some more company? At least that's

125

how David translated the torrent of Spanish, for they were both speaking at once. Naturally we invited them in, and lo and behold, Gaspar was actually *gay*, and so while I lay sideways on the massage table with my head off the edge and my legs in the air so I could suck David while José fucked me, I could watch Boyfriend finally getting *his* cock sucked by Gaspar, whose black, glittering Mayan eyes closed in concentration, and I howled with not simply orgasm but the *excitement*, the splendid excitement of being in Mexico in a bathhouse with four uncut men and a maniac, a place no woman I knew had gone before. Steam swirled in the saturated air like superheated fog, beading like pearls in the web of a huge Yucatán spider in the corner; David's cock, or was it José's or Carlos's again, I didn't care, pounded my fully opened cunt rhythmically and I wished I had her view.

You know if you have ever been to a bathhouse that time stands still in the steamy, throbbing air, and so I had no idea how long it went on, only that sometimes I was on my back and sometimes on my knees, and once for a minute I was standing facing the wall, and when Boyfriend wasn't sucking them or fucking me, he was taking snapshots of us, just like a tourist. The floor of the room was completely littered with condoms, which made us all laugh hysterically. Rubber-kneed, Gaspar and David held me up with Carlos and José flanking them so Boyfriend could snap one last picture. Then he divided all the rest of the condoms among them – we had more at the hotel, I think that week we went through ten dozen – and got out his brochures. He was trying to explain in Spanish the little condoms he used for giving head – how great they were to use with uncut guys 'cause they disappeared under the foreskin – and I was asking David what it was like to live a double life, Riverside High to Los

Baños, and who else came there – "Oh, everybody does," he said – and did they ever want to fuck him – of course they *wanted* to – and did he ever fuck them – well, sure – and how was that? He shrugged and said, as if there were only one possible response to my question, "It's *fucking*."

When we left, the moon was high, the Baños deserted, the warm night air almost cool after the steamy room. The place looked like a courtyard motel, the kind I used to stay in with my parents when we travelled in the early sixties, but overgrown and haunted. The Pan figure glittered in the low lobby light, and the man at the desk charged us $35 – seven for each massage boy, four each to get in, and six for the room. Hundreds of thousands of pesos – he looked anxious, as though he feared we'd think it was too much. We paid him, laughing. I wondered if this was how a Japanese businessman in Thailand felt. Was I contributing to the imperialist decline of the third world? Boyfriend didn't give a shit about things like that, so I didn't mention it. In my hand was a crumpled note from David: 'Can I come visit you in your hotel room? No money.'

Falling for Holden

Sean Condon

Sean Condon is the author of *Sean & David's Long Drive* and *Drive Thru America*, published by Lonely Planet.

I don't even know what the hell I was doing in New York anyway, if you want to know the truth. I don't even like the place that much. It's too big and confusing and sometimes you never know *who* the hell you are. All I know for sure is that I fell in love with her right away and pretty soon after *that* I ended up in here, where I'm supposed to be taking it easy for a while.

I'm gonna skip all that David Copperfield kind of crap about where I was born and what my lousy childhood was like and all. In the first place it's just *not* that interesting, and in the second place there's already a whole bunch of *other* goddam embarrassing stuff that I have to admit to anyway. I wish like hell I didn't, but I do. I really do.

You've probably guessed by now that I've read *The Catcher in the Rye*. I've read it about two thousand times in fact. I just keep on reading it. I can't help it – the goddam thing just keeps on showing up and I keep on reading it. I was even reading it just recently when I was in New York that day when I met this girl. It was right in my back pocket.

It was cold that day. Not snowing-cold, but breath-cold. You could see your breath if you breathed out real hard. I was breathing like a goddam asthmatic, partly because I'm a pretty heavy smoker and partly because I'd been running around Madison and 75th all over the place looking for the Whitney Museum which I couldn't find anywhere. I could've *sworn* they'd moved it since last time I was here. That's the thing with New York – it has simple blocks and straight grids everywhere but it always seems different every time you go there. Like they've changed it around a little bit while you weren't looking.

If you start out from just *slightly* the wrong place you can end up getting lost forever. Anyway, I'd just about given up and was lighting my millionth cigarette of the day when out of nowhere this big stupid St Bernard leaped up on me and knocked me flat on my back. All of a sudden I was lying on the sidewalk looking up at the sky. I was pretty surprised. You don't see too many unleashed dogs in the city, especially ones as big as that goddam St Bernard. But I didn't really mind because he was a pretty friendly bastard and was slobbering all over me in that dog way while I lay there only *pretending* to fend him off. If I really *wanted* to I could've fended him off easily. I'm a pretty good fender, if you want to know the truth. And in a way, I think that crazy St Bernard knew that.

Anyway, a minute later I heard a voice crying, "Laddy! Laddy!" and some very rapid footsteps clacking and echoing all over the place. And before I had time to get up and brush myself off, this girl was standing right over me with an empty leash in one hand and a Styrofoam skull in the other. And boy, she was beautiful.

She was the kind of beautiful where you can't speak because you wouldn't know what the hell to say to a girl like that if you had a million years to think about it. Two million even. And at the same time you knew you *had* to think of something to say or you'd never see her again and you didn't even want to *think* about what your life would be like if you never saw her again. It's not a great situation to find yourself in *ever*, let alone with a big dog lying right on top of you.

So there we were, Laddy and me lying on the sidewalk and her looking down at us. Everything was silent except for old Laddy's hot, noisy slobbering. It felt like we could stay that way for years when all of a sudden she broke the spell by smiling this gorgeous smile. I was free. I could speak.

I pushed the dog off me and stood up. And right away, because she'd smiled that terrific smile, I could think of hundreds of things to say. Unfortunately, I said just about the stupidest thing anybody could say right at that moment. I pointed to the goddam foam skull she was carrying and said, "So did ya know Yorick *well*, or did ya just *know* him?"

Boy, I was really showing off with that crack. Even to tell you exactly *how* I was showing off sounds like showing off but unfortunately I have to or it doesn't make any sense. What it is, in the play *Hamlet* everybody thinks it's, 'Alas, poor Yorick. I knew him well.' But it's not. It's actually, 'Alas! Poor Yorick. I knew him, *Horatio*.' So that was how I was showing off. I hate having to remember it and tell you about it but that was the way it happened.

It didn't matter anyway because she began laughing her head off as though it was the funniest goddam thing she'd ever heard. She may have even been laughing *at* me for being such a show-off. I'm not sure because I forgot to ask her about it later. She had a beautiful laugh too. Some people have terrible laughs, all loud and horsey, or it sounds like it comes from their nose or something. But not her. Her laugh was like music. I know that's a terrible cliché, but it's true. When she laughed that day it was like beautiful music and light fog rising from her mouth into the cold.

After that I didn't waste too much time before finding out her name and if she lacked a boyfriend and seeing whether she might be interested in meeting me for a cocktail that evening. I was pouring on the charm. I can be quite charming when I'm in the right mood and I was really pouring it on. Frances said she'd be delighted. *Delighted.* It kills me when somebody says they'd be delighted to do something. Especially if it's something I've suggested. Even more if I've suggested a date with me.

Boy, I was so excited I could hardly stand it. As soon as I got back to my crumby little room at the Edmont Hotel, I started calling up all my friends back in Montreal, where I live, and telling them that they should start packing and come to New York right away because I was going to get married in a day or two. I actually *told* them I was getting married. That's how excited I was. I even called my mother to tell her the big news. The thing was, all of them had heard that kind of stuff from me a number of times before, so mostly they just kind of laughed and said, "Yeah, sure. See you soon." They said it in a nice way, of course, but it still depressed the hell out of me that everybody found me so unreliable. Or predictable.

I wore my best suit. The *only* suit I had with me to be completely accurate, but it was still a hell of a nice suit. I always travel with a good suit because you never know if you're going to meet somebody where you need to wear a suit. It's terrible if you can't represent yourself properly in the right clothes. I'm not particularly handsome, but I do like to make the best of things by wearing nice clothes. I have to admit that I had a pretty nice tie and shoes as well.

Anyway, we met that night at this little hole-in-the-wall-type bar on Houston St called Molino's. It's not particularly swanky or anything but they have this terrific jukebox there and I always feel a whole lot more comfortable if I'm surrounded by music I like.

Frances arrived right on time and waved to me when she walked in. She actually *waved* to me in a bar. I damn near fell off my chair when she did that. It was so corny and sweet. She sat down opposite me and put her face so close to mine I thought

she was gonna kiss me. But all she did was say, "Well hello."
Then she said something that really threw me. She said, "You
know, I don't even know your name."

Right away I knew I was in trouble. I mean she looked
absolutely terrific in this fur hat and one of those furry hand-
warmer things. Not too many people could get away with stuff
like that but old Frances pulled it off like a pro. So I didn't really
know what to say because of how great she looked. And I have
a really bad name. Not like a criminal *record* name but one that
just sounds dumb. Like it doesn't really belong to me.

"Uh . . . Holden. Please to meetcha," I said and shook her hand
like a real cornball. I didn't want her to say anything about the
name so right away I asked her what she was in the mood to
drink. I got up from the table in such a hurry that I almost
knocked the goddam thing over. "I'm gonna have a scotch and
soda, you want one of those?" I said. "They're really very good.
If you like them and all. I'll get us a coupla those, whaddaya
say?" She nodded and I got the hell away from her as fast as I
could.

I calmed down after a few more drinks and quit acting like
such a madman. Not that she seemed to mind me hyperventilat-
ing all over the place. I was talking about a hundred miles an
hour too. All 'goddam' this and 'phoney' that. It was quite a feat,
I can tell you. I even asked her if she knew where the goddam
ducks from Central Park go in winter. I really did. And I have to
tell you, she loved it. God, she was a nice kid though. And
interesting as hell too.

She lived with her folks in Manhattan and was studying
medicine and psychiatry, which was why she was carrying that
crazy skull. Before that she'd attended Dana Hall, which, in case
you never heard of it, is a very exclusive school. But she wasn't

all snooty about it either. She didn't think it was the biggest deal on earth that she went to this very exclusive school. You take most people who go to a school like that, they think the rest of us have to start worshipping them right away. She didn't though. I don't even know why she mentioned it in the first place. I probably asked.

Somewhere in our conversation way up the back in the dark of old Molino's, Frances told me this great story from when she was little. How she'd gone to this kind of holiday camp at her school for the day where they just had fun playing games and all. This was when she was about seven or eight years old. That crazy age where you don't know what's going on – the bad stuff at least. Anyway, they spent the first morning inside a classroom and all the kids had to take their shoes off to keep the floor nice or something. When they got let out at lunchtime old Frances left her shoes inside and the teacher had locked the door to the classroom. So she just wandered around the playground in her white socks doing laps of the concrete ring that circled the grassy sports field, all crying and miserable and too scared to ask to get her shoes back. Her socks became all dirty because she didn't even take them off. That story damn near broke my heart, I can tell you. I was laughing when she told me but sort of crying in my mind at the same time. It killed me. It really did.

So then I started telling her some stories from when I was a kid. Only they weren't *my* stories. They were straight out of *The Catcher in the* goddam *Rye*. I told her about me and Jane Gallagher playing checkers that summer in Maine and my little brother Allie's baseball mitt and how I went crazy after he died and all sorts of other stuff. Fighting with Ward Stradlater in the dorm and pretending my name was Rudolf Schmidt to this lady I'd met on a train. Boy, I was on fire. I gave her the works. She just sat there listening to me in the most beautiful way you could imagine. Her eyes were on me the whole time. I could tell that she really liked me. But it wasn't just that she was watching me, you could tell that she could see in her imagination everything I was telling her about. I could too, to tell you the truth. It was all pretty vivid and believable.

Then all the really bad stuff happened. I'd just finished telling Frances about my little sister Phoebe and this record I'd bought for her and how I broke it, and I guess I must have looked kind of teary because although I don't even *have* a little sister called Phoebe and it didn't actually *happen* to me, it was still pretty upsetting. Anyway, I must have looked upset because right then Frances put her hand over mine and said, "Oh Holden, please don't cry." Boy, I was finished after she said that.

I started bawling like a madman – the real kind, not the kind you get in literature – and trying to explain that my name wasn't really Holden and that none of the stuff I'd told her about was real. That I was just some regular idiot on a stupid holiday going crazy from being all alone in a city the size of New York. I could tell that she was quite confused and bothered by all of it. In fact, it probably annoyed the hell out of her, but I had to confess. I liked her way too much to go on pretending. I still wanted to *marry* her, for Christ's sake. I guess I must've been shouting by that time because she kept telling me to keep my voice down. But I can't remember too well.

Anyway, by the time I'd finished telling her about all that David Copperfield kind of crap – the *real* David Copperfield kind of crap about who I *really* was and what my not particularly lousy childhood was *actually* like – Frances looked kind of exhausted. And a little bored. She shook her head and said, "It's such a shame. I liked you so much. The *other* you." I could've died.

But I didn't die, I just sort of disappeared. As though I'd fallen off the edge of a great field where I'd been playing and there was no one around to catch me.

Ramadan

Mona Simpson

Mona Simpson was born in Green Bay, Wisconsin, in 1957. Recently selected as one of Granta's best young American novelists, she is the author of *Anywhere But Here*, *The Lost Father* and *A Regular Guy*. Her short stories have appeared in *Harper's*, *Granta*, the *Paris Review* and *Ploughshares*.

W elcome in Egypt," a large man said.

Egypt, that first brass afternoon in spring, may have been the most stylish place I ever saw on the earth. Nobody had ever told me about the cars. The cars were old German and American models from the fifties and sixties, black and rounded. They honked and shined everywhere, and I found a driver to Alexandria with my guidebook propped between two pronged fingers like a piece of music. Alexandria was a long way – two guys turned me down before this one. He was handsome and young, with many teeth, and he had a dry grassy smell the closer I stood to him. We bargained a price in dollars. I still had to get pounds. He knew almost no English. He had a book. I sat in the back of the old Mercedes on deep leather seats made soft with time and watched out of the rolled-down windows as we left Cairo in a circle like a maze and drove north into the horizon of cypresses, eucalyptus and olive trees. It was good.

There was so much sky. The ground and trees, people and even buildings rose about an inch and the rest was sky. It was 24 February. I wanted to remember the day. I lay my head back on the seat and the smell of earth rolled over me. This wasn't desert as I'd expected. It was dirt, not light sand; the vegetation was scarce and sombre. Ragged trees moved slightly in the soft wind, and they seemed to whine and creak. Date palm and sycamore. Closer in, there were acacia, juniper, jacaranda and grass.

I felt looser in my clothes when I couldn't see Cairo behind us any more. We were on an old road. The structures you saw in the distance looked small, made of concrete and mud. A rich weedy taste came through the air. I thought of my father and how, even though he was a boy who grew up here in this old slow country, he'd moved in suits and silk ties all over the world. I'd travelled too. I'd driven cross-country, had my college summer in Europe; even my grandmother, in Wisconsin, had been around the world. But do we, any of us, love more?

*

If this was Egypt, maybe that explained Wisconsin. His existence there. On the road ahead of us I saw a small lake and then a mountain, which disappeared when we came close. I'd been told about mirages in school, when I learned the word, but I'd never seen one. Maybe it took a desert to produce them. Once in a while the driver turned to me and we'd try to talk but it was too hard, so he'd fall back to driving, which he did with an evenness and a happy hum that seemed as odd and discordant as sitar music. He had a vague smile which seemed to move through a sort of plot sequence. I rested back on the seat, thinking how I'd like to sleep with this boy just once, tonight, in my hotel room and wondering if I could, how this worked and whether I should give him money. This was so foreign no one would know. No one ever. For the rest of my life no one would know.

I stared at the back of his neck. His hair was cut short but it still curled. Below the line of hair were two lines of sweat, tiny drops balanced on the dark taut skin. At that moment I thought how hard it was to be a man. The distance between imagining and placing a hand in the world on to someone's skin – I didn't know how that happened. That seemed enormous. Even when there were two cultures and no language and you had the money. But no. That wasn't good. Being bought with money could harm anyone.

I tapped his shoulder – his skin through the cotton was warm – and pointed for him to stop at a market, a bazaar of some kind by the side of the road. It looked like a farm food stand anywhere in America, except the trees were high date palms. I was hungry. He pulled over the Mercedes, its bulk calming smoothly on the dirt gravel pass. We got out. The canvas- and tin-roofed tents shaded jars of oil, dates still on the branch, almonds, pine nuts, diamond-cut pastries in tin pans that ran with honey, hazed by close thick black flies, pomegranates, olives, figs open and red, dusty purple on the outside. A thin man, dark-skinned with almost no hair on his legs and arms and head, sat cross-legged on a striped rug on the uneven ground. His eyes were nearly closed. A clear glass jar, like one you would buy jam in, sat full by his knee. I tried to get close. I browsed by a table with nothing recognisable on it, some kind of cheese in water, I thought. I saw then in his jar: a coiled snake; I couldn't tell dead or alive.

I wanted figs, dates and almonds and started to gather them in a brown paper bag, but my driver came up and with elaborate arm motions pointed to his chest, establishing, I'll do this, without words. The thin man's flat sunken mouth smiled a big smile. He tried to take her and was caught. She's an American, it's all game.

Walking back to the car with my bag of fruit, I heard a familiar monotonous sound. I walked across the sand and looked behind the tent. A rickety ping-pong table was set up on the ground and two dark boys were playing. Then we were driving again, and he conducted a long speech to me in Arabic, probably about how much money he'd saved me, and I murmured something to make it seem I understood. 'Is no good for you, is better for you', was all I made out from his speech. His one arm sometimes lifted off the wheel, articulate and graceful, but I wished I could settle it back to driving and I ate the fresh dates, the skins crumbling like sugar and the fruit inside melting like honey. I could eat like this for a hundred years. In the back seat there was a long soft breeze and sun on the left side, so I took off my shoes and my long shirt and just lay down in my tank top and skirt, legs bare, feet on the leather, feeling it almost like another skin. I was sort of asleep but not really. The breeze played on my belly, my upper arms, the bones of my neck. It was good. The smell of the fruit on the foot-space swelled up in shells of air.

Before I left, I'd wanted to find some Arabs to write things down for me. I stopped at the place across from the school that sold hummus and tabouli and shish kebab in pita. But the guys there turned out to be Israelis. Nice guys. They gave me a felalel and suggested that I check the university. It would have to have some kind of Arab Studies department.

I asked directions and went upstairs. On a third floor corner, I found Near Eastern Studies. A woman in black jeans and a black turtle-neck stood near a floor-to-ceiling wire cage which held a parrot. Inside the cage, which looked home-made, was a large, driftwood branch where the parrot perched. The woman held a finger to the bird. From the glint of jewel, I saw she was married. She was dark-skinned, wide-eyed, with an extremely full, flower-shaped mouth. She sounded younger than she looked.

"I'm Mayan Atassi." That was the first time I'd said it since Ted Stevenson broke our names and then returned to random-ness. "I'm looking for someone Egyptian."

The parrot flapped its long wings and squawked. She laughed. "Egyptian. Let's see. Professor Kamal is," she said, "but he's on leave in Paris this year."

"You're not Egyptian?" I said.

"No, I'm from Lebanon," she said. My whole life I'd heard of Beirut and how it was the Switzerland of the Middle East. I knew that I had been conceived there.

"Do you know Arabic?"

"Yes, mmhmm."

I began to explain. My mother never wanted me to be alone with my dad. "He could have you on a plane to Egypt in ten minutes," she'd snap her fingers, "and they'd have you married off and swelled up pregnant at fourteen. That's what they do to girls over there. Girls are nothing."

"What about going to college?" I'd said.

"College, in Egypt?" she said. She burst out with a bitter-rinded laugh. "Forget it."

I was grown up now and being pregnant didn't seem only shame. It appeared even beautiful, a common thing. It was strange having outlived the life with my mother: I was forever rediscovering little things that I had believed and assumed and were not true. Anyway, I might never be able to get pregnant and that was because of me. I'd dieted too much when I was in high school.

On three sheets of paper, the woman with the parrot wrote in Arabic the Station Street address, my address in America, and a little paragraph that I dictated saying who I was and that I was looking for my father whom I hadn't seen in years, and his name. I looked at her ring while she wrote. It was dark gold, the diamond capped on either side by bright blue-green gems cut in squares.

I opened my wallet and slipped the three papers in the deepest part. They became treasures. She asked me if I would come back when I returned and tell her what happened.

I was halfway down the hall, a clean echoing hall of black

tiles, and then I ran back. "Do you know what the weather is like there?"

She stepped out from behind the desk. She was a plump-cheeked woman, big breasted, wonderful looking. "Nice. Perfect. Like your San Francisco."

*

Some time later he made a punctuating noise in the front and I sat up. I saw Alexandria in the distance, like a series of half staircases on a hill. This was the place my father grew up. It was early evening, seven o'clock and not much light. The roads (some of them) looked older than the Ottoman empire but were still used, not kept for antique. There were geraniums in the windows, like Paris. The stone and plaster were crumbling and dirty. A lot of the houses had clay pots on the roofs. I wondered why. Some of the buildings had a white sheen, with mosaic. The streets were quieter than Cairo, the neighbourhoods lower, the old sun like a bucket full of water spilled on the bricks. This was a smaller city, I guessed, and was supposed to be holy. I knew that. Not only for me.

"*Mumkin ahgiz ohda ghur-fa min hi-na?*"

I read to him from the guidebook but he didn't understand. Then I gave up and moved behind his shoulder and showed him where it was printed in Arabic calligraphy, pointing with my fingernail while the car moved unevenly over the bricks. I wanted a hotel. He put his hand to his forehead, and then exploded in head-nodding. He was so young. His shirt was striped, yellow and green. Just then I noticed a band aid on his right arm, near the elbow, a band aid printed with circus animals, the kind we always wanted as children. Is that what became of circus band aids? The surplus shipped to the Third World?

We turned a corner and beyond us was the Mediterranean, blue and green and moving with unrest, a sea of barking dogs. He drove me to an ugly hotel, modern and run-down. I said no, crossed my arms, and found the word for old in the guidebook. This made him think a moment and then he got it, and the next place was right: white and Persian-looking, with small cracks snaking down the towers. He parked the Mercedes, pulled the keys out and came inside with me, carrying the pack. It seemed too hard to argue. He wanted to deal with the desk for me, so I stood next to him, holding out my credit card. The man behind the desk took it, produced a key and that was the end of it. An old cage elevator, with script I could not read, lyrical cursives strewn in fancy metal painted white, stopped at the ninth floor where the smell of old geraniums came profuse and dusty and breath-stopping almost: I followed and he opened the door of my room and it was good.

French doors opened to a small terrace and the sunset fired outside. I looked in the bathroom: it was completely tiled, even the ceiling. You could wash it out with a hose. The bed was plain and white; a small prayer rug waited in one corner. The carpet was a very faded red, and dirty.

My driver put my backpack down and stood there.

I pulled my wallet out of the pack and paid him the amount we agreed plus ten dollars.

He counted slowly, with complication, twice, then his face cleared and he handed me back ten one dollar bills.

I shook my head no, pointed – for you – then I grabbed the phrase book and tried to find the words that meant 'for the children'. In the guidebook, it said you were supposed to say 'for the children'. He looked pretty young to have children and I couldn't find the damn phrase anyway, so I pushed the money back into his hand and he shook his head no, and I put my hands behind my back meaning I won't take it and then he pushed my shoulders, gentle but a real push, the money held up in his hand between us, and for a minute we didn't know what was happening and then we were falling back, first me on the bed and then him.

His skin stretched and spread taut wings from his neck to his top chest bones. I remembered that he was young, probably younger than twenty. I wanted to hear his name. I didn't want it to be Atassi. He could have been. My father might have come back. Then I remembered my father telling me around the old kitchen table, "If I went back, I'd be running the country. I was the John F. Kennedy of Egypt." Well, he wasn't running the country. I read the newspapers. I knew those people's names. He said so little to us that I saved every sentence. I could lift one up like a bracelet or strand of pearls from a box. As if any young man could be held responsible for grandiose dreams whispered to an infant daughter, when he was new in a country and still thought everything was possible.

But he could have come back. It was more than twenty years ago he'd said that. He was a very young man then.

I rolled over on my belly, reached down for the guidebook. My shoes fell off the side of the bed. He pulled me back by my ankle. I felt his fingers like a bracelet. I rifled through the pages. There it was: My name is _____ . "Ismee Mayan Atassi," I said.

He pointed to his chest. "Ramazan el-Said. I was born during the Ramadan, so my mother called me that."

OK. Fine. I lay back on the bed; the book dropped. This was good. We couldn't say a word and I'd stopped trying, but maybe because of that something else worked. I always talked too much in bed anyway. I lay back and wished he would touch my neck for some reason, I don't know why, and I don't know if I'd ever wanted that or thought that before, my neck, but he did, first with his fingers, hard so I felt my pulse flutter. I didn't know if it would be different or the same so far away with someone not in my language, a complete stranger, but I watched the fan in the ceiling slowly mark the room with carousel shadows and in a minute I was lifting my hips to shrug my skirt off and then we were both naked, he was dark and thin and not different really. I touched him and looked in his face, his cheeks seemed to spread wider apart and questions stood like cool statues in his eyes and I wanted him and started it and then it began. It went on a long time, well into first dark, it never really stopped. I'd turn over on my side and clutch some sheet around me and look out of the windows at the clear stars and he'd be on my back with his hands and mouth and then something would feel like a shot, absolute and four-pointed but blooming pleasure and we'd begin again and it went on so long sometimes I'd forget. I'd feel I was the man, entering him, and he seemed that way too, opened, split, eyes shallowing up like hungry fish on the surface, as if in the night we traded who owned the outside and the inside, who could penetrate and who could enclose. The stranger was in me and I wanted that. I finally fell asleep. He woke me and I heard water rushing. It was still dark. I dragged the sheet behind me to the window, where there was one star that almost hurt to look at, a too proud diamond, somebody else's, and I wondered why he'd woken me so late or so early, and then he pushed me to the bathroom where he'd run a deep tub with a flower floating on the top. The whole thing smelled almond and he put me in it. I saw blood. It wavered in the water like a frilly ribbon. I stepped out and saw him kneeling by the bed. The sheet was soaked red.

I was bleeding. He started kissing the inside of my thighs, which were blood-stained like some all-directional flower. I couldn't tell him how happy I was with the guidebook; there was no way to explain. Before I lost my period, like a stitch in knitting, I'd minded blood in a prissy way, hated the bother of it, worried about spotting. Now I could have tasted it. I felt like shouting. That was over, the long punishment for what I'd done to myself. I had my choices again. He was looking up at me now with different eyes, submissive. He knelt by the bed and capped my knees with his hands. He said words I didn't know.

Then he rampaged through the room. I found him squatting over the guidebook. He said in English, I love you. He kept looking up at me in this slave way. Then I understood. The blood. He thought that meant virgin, that I'd given that to him. "No," I tried to tell him. "No." He picked me up, an arm under the crook of my knees and one under my back. He took me to the tub again. He was carrying me like a fragile child. I had to clear this up. But there was no way. His brown eyes fixed. I slipped down into the water, and heard him in the other room pulling up his pants, the clink of keys and change. He stole out of the door. I figured I'd never see him again and that was fine, like a sealed perfect envelope. A tangerine peeled, every section intact. I got up out of the water to latch the door behind him. Then I went back to sleep, thrilling even in dream every time I felt the trickle of blood.

*

The next morning, I felt proud because with the guidebook I ordered room service coffee and it came with a wet rose on the table-clothed tray. The petals fell off easily when I pulled because the flower was full and seedy. Outside, the hills were raw brown with a haze of purple on the surface. The ocean was a plain grey colour. I took a bath and remembered the night. I sat with the coffee on the tiled rim of the tub. A line of blood ran jagged like the thinnest twig. The blood was going to be a problem. I called the desk and sat with the guidebook and finally sputtered 'Tampax' in English. The man said, "Oh, Tampax," and a few minutes later the elevator creaked and a boy appeared with a blue unopened box on a cloth-covered tray with a new rose. I put on a white shirt, brushed on mascara and left.

His car was parked across the street. The sight hit me like a sling. I tiptoed up: he was asleep on the back seat. He looked pathetic. He was too big for the car, and he slept with one leg folded under him and his head bent against the window. I left him be and walked downhill to ask directions at a fruit stand. I waited my turn. The high citrus smell tickled my face and behind the server two towers of orange and lemon hulls hovered. I showed him my scrap of paper with the Station Street address that the woman with the parrot had written, and he pointed. I wanted to buy lemonade but I remembered I hadn't changed my money. I started walking.

I passed a movie theatre with calligraphy on the marquee. The photographs by the ticket booth showed a huge Omar Sharif, older now, with salt and pepper hair. I had seen all his movies. I had wondered whether he was even still alive. He was never in anything any more. But his career hadn't fallen to ruins. He was here.

I heard birds as I climbed the winding streets and I smelled myrtle and sage. There was also the distant hammer sound of construction. I hadn't expected the whirring of bicycles everywhere. They were black and old, like the cars. After a few minutes outside I was used to camels. I'd stopped and touched the black lips of one, wet and soft, gumming my hand. Then I felt something nudge my hip. It was the Mercedes. At first I was mad. I twisted my skirt to see if it had made a mark. He sat at the wheel, grinning, motioning me to get in. I didn't see what else I could do, so I got in the front seat, giving up my adventure but glad anyway. I showed him the Station Street address.

He put a hand, softly, on my lower belly. I wriggled away. But it was good he found me. He studied a map and it took us fifteen minutes of turns and curves, in opposite directions. Then we were at the house.

It still stood. A tall straggly eucalyptus waited in front. It was a wooden and concrete house, three floors with two balconies, brownish coloured with old rusty metal and stucco. The roof was red tile, Spanish looking. I saw a metal drain-pipe like the one at home. The eucalyptus moved in the wind above me. I wanted to get rid of the driver. I didn't know how long I would be. I didn't want anyone waiting for me.

I returned to the car, knocked on the window and motioned to him wildly, to say it could be a long time. He pointed to his chest, then to the floor of the car. I guess he meant that he'd be there. I shrugged, tapping my watch. I spread out my hand wide. Eternity. He folded his arms and closed his eyes.

*

The sky was clear blue with no clouds and I heard the drift of a slight wind in the eucalyptus leaves, a tired and very old sound. Patience, they seemed to whisper, patience. Summer is long. My heart beat like something flung against a wall. There was no bell, and I knocked. A wind chime of crude glass and metal pipes hung from the eaves. Nobody answered. The porch was cool, clay-tiled. I knocked again.

I checked my slip of paper against the number on the door. Yes, twenty-two was the number. Outside the door was an old orange plastic chair and on the ground, the dish for a plant, filled with what looked like rain-water. I heard a window shoved open in the house next door to the right, and a woman's hot fast voice spilled through and I said, "Isam Atassi. American." There was a noise inside her building of feet on a staircase. A door whipped open and the woman stood there looking me over.

She crossed her arms firmly over her substantial chest and spoke to me, her head shaking. The only words I recognised were 'no America, no America'. For a moment I thought she was trying to chase me away but then she was showing me into her house with her arms, almost bowing, big loops of arm hanging down like stretching dough from shoulder to elbow, from elbow to hand. She stood with her ample back to me, hands on hips, calling up the stairs; a little girl ran down, a round-limbed blue-eyed blonde. The woman said something to the child, and the child gathered her skirts in both fists and started running. "No America," the woman said again, this time bending in a near curtsy. I finally got it; she didn't speak English. She motioned me to sit and I did. She sat across from me and folded her hands on her lap and her feet one behind the other. I couldn't help noticing her legs. Her calves were enormous, over the dainty gesture of her feet, and patterns of black hair were trapped under her nylon stockings. Then she sprang up, graceful and light, and slowly lifted the lid off a green cut-glass bowl of candy. To be polite I took one. It was a date wrapped around nuts, and rolled in sugar and ground pistachio. It was good. She slowly panto-mimed drinking from a glass, then lifted her eyebrows to ask if

I wanted anything. I shook my head no, not wanting to get into a beverage charade.

We sat politely in the still living room on fancy maroon velvet couches with gold tassels, our hands folded, looking in different directions. She smiled at me every few moments. After a long while the girl skidded in with a boy who might have been her brother but didn't look like it. They were calling back and forth in avid musical conversation. The boy stood before the woman, probably his grandmother, hands at his sides and chin down, awaiting an order. More fast Arabic. I rested with the ease of understanding absolutely nothing.

Then the boy turned to face me and said, "I know English."

"Oh, good," I said, loudly. "Are you learning in school?"

"Yes," he said. "School."

"What is your name?" I said.

"My name is Nauras Awafti."

I reached out my hand. "My name is Mayan Atassi."

"Yes. There are many here," the boy said.

The grandmother became impatient and pulled the boy to her by the back of his shirt. He turned and translated for her. She fired questions at him hard and fast. Then he swivelled back to me. She smiled, and showed her teeth, some of them not white, and lifted her old plump hand in a wave.

"I am American," I said. "My mother is American, my father is from here. Egyptian. He grew up next door. My father is Mohammed Atassi and I came here to find him."

"Mohammed ah-yah," the old woman said, her head going up and down. The boy translated what I had said.

"He left my mother years ago. I haven't seen my father – Mohammed – since I was twelve years old." I marked the height with my hand. "Around your age. I wonder if you, or your grandmother, know where he is."

He grinned and said, "She's not my grandmother," as if this were a hilarious mistake. I hoped to hell she was not his mother. "She's my grandmother's sister. My grandmother's upstairs." He pointed to the ceiling.

The old woman grabbed his collar again sternly to get him back to business.

"Does she know where my father is?" I repeated.

She shook her head and I knew my answer even before he translated.

"You come all the way from America to find him?" the boy said.

"Yes," I said. The woman closed her eyes and continued rocking her head.

She spoke and the boy translated. "He hasn't been there for a long time. Not thirty years. She says he's somewhere in America. When his father die, next door, he wasn't at funeral. You have bad luck because they live there next door, Farhan's wife and daughter. But they went for two months already to America."

America. I was astonished. "Where in America?" I said.

She shrugged.

"She says she doesn't know. But she thinks California."

I looked at the little blonde girl. She was sitting in a big chair, her arms clutched to the armrests, her round legs ending in blunted sneakers. She stared up at me, the American.

The boy said that my father's mother was very old but still in the house next door. He asked if I would like to meet her.

I thought I'd heard the translation wrong. "Yes!" I said. "Yes!" My other grandmother.

The old woman spoke and the boy said that she had invited me to eat a meal with them first. She stood up, with her huge knees facing out, bent them in a *plié* and lifted and spread her arms to encompass the room. The woman's repertoire of gestures belonged to a clown. A fat clown. I liked her very much. I appreciated her exaggerated courtesies, but I wanted to go. I tapped my watch and pointed at the house next door. I was sick of people – even Egyptians, even neighbours – who saw my father once thirty years ago. I didn't want strangers. I had a grandmother locked in the house next door.

The old woman rose, negotiated her weight around the furniture and motioned me with a plump fluid wrist to follow. The kids stood on either side of me, looking at me as if I were the strangest being they'd ever seen. We went through a mint-green kitchen, like an old-fashioned one at home, and out of the back door. The backyard went far. Three goats faced us. There was a chicken coop too, with loud dirty-white chickens. From a eucalyptus tree, an old tyre hung and the lawn was worn smooth and grassless. Past the yard and a shed was a field, just weeds, down the hill to a stand of olive trees. I knew my father must have run there.

I could have stayed. But the woman and the boy and girl were entering the next house's back door and I followed. We walked into a cellar full of vegetables and fruit in clear jars, cans with faded labels, jars of honey and vats of olive oil and sacks of grain. I picked up a jar of olives that were still attached to their branch. The woman tapped at a jar that contained something like yellow peanut butter. Her lips opened on her teeth in a large expression that strained for meaning. "Mohammed," she said, and moved a hand on her ample belly.

The boy translated. "He liked that for his meal every day." I didn't know what it was.

We entered a kitchen that looked as if it had been remodelled twenty years before, in matching black and white checks. The cupboards seemed safe and ample, the corners rounded, the surfaces used and worn. It was clean and plain. We passed into a large living room with plush emerald-green carpeting and fancy satin and velvet couches and chairs. Gold ropes marked off parts of the room. An old inlaid chess table and some brass trays looked Middle Eastern; the mahogany console stand holding an RCA colour television could have been anywhere. I stopped at some chrome-framed pictures on a shelf. The photographs showed a wedding. The bride was a full, young, curly-haired girl who looked nothing like me. There were eight pictures of her sitting in her flower-decked throne and in each one she was wearing a different dress. My father was not there. The old woman shook her head sadly, with raised eyebrows. "Mohammed, no," she said.

We climbed upstairs, the children ahead. The woman ascended slowly, holding the gold velvet rope that served as a banister. On the first landing, there was a family room, with another sofa and chairs, a book shelf, a standing globe, and corridors leading to more bedrooms. We started up the second stairs. Near the top, the woman called the children back. She explained something to the boy and he ran ahead, two steps at a time, arms scissoring with purpose.

We entered the top room. A young woman with her hair held back pressed by us out of the door. She stood on the landing, holding one elbow. She was wearing a nurse's uniform with a long zipper. It was a wide, low-ceilinged room, pink and white in the eaves. Outside, eucalyptus leaves fingered the window panes. The room was full of roses, their petals falling from the night table on to table-tops, the floor, the lush satin bedspread. There she was, rising from a chair with great effort, collapsing down again, an old woman with a deeply lined dark face, a mouth large as a harmonica, with many teeth and a puff of white hair. Her eyes were clear blue. She was large and short.

"Momo," she said, her whole face crumbling over the words. She hugged me and she smelled a way I hadn't ever known an old woman to smell, warmly sweet like caramel. We sat in white, satin-cushioned chairs and the boy translated between us. She had a clear sad look when she shook her head after the boy asked if she knew where her youngest son was. She had not heard from him for ten years, she said. Her eyebrows lifted and her large mouth formed a beautiful shape. She told the boy she had not seen him for almost twenty. She lifted her hands and I went close and knelt down so she could hold my face.

She told us that when my father was a boy he liked the animals. He was always out in the air with animals. I asked if he had been smart. She shrugged, frowning, then slowly nodded her head to say that she supposed so.

I moved to the small attic window. I could see the field and the goats. My father had run there, a boy like any boy. There was a muddy pen. A sandbox. The woman from next door tilted her head and made a gesture that we should let the old woman rest.

I knelt and kissed her goodbye. We walked out and she called us back in words I didn't recognise. She'd lifted herself up and got to a bureau. From the top drawer, open now, I saw a thousand things – threads, thimbles, scissors, papers, cards, scarves, veils, stockings, lipsticks, jewellery. She extracted a tiny photograph of my father, about an inch square, black and white with a white ruffled edge.

She gave it to me and I closed my hand around it. I couldn't look at it until later. In the cellar again, the woman from next door gave me the jar of what my father had liked. She pointed to the ceiling.

"She wanted you to have," the boy said.

*

Before I left I gave them the scrap of paper where the woman with the parrot had written my address. "You can visit me in America someday," I said.

"*Inshallah,*" the boy said. He copied the address down and returned the paper to me.

I asked him what the word meant in Arabic. I'd heard it all around me.

"God willing," the boy said, "in Egypt nothing for sure. Everything is *inshallah*."

I asked him what my name meant.

"It's just a name like other names. A common name here."

"I thought it meant light," I said. That's what my parents had told me.

"No. Nora means light."

"What about Amneh?" That was my middle name. I thought it meant to wish.

"No. Believer."

I hoped that Ramazan was still outside and we could drive back to Cairo. He would rub my back and I would fly home into the dawn. I wanted to leave. I felt like a person who had thrown a diamond ring down off a bridge and watched it disappear into the dark water. It was over, I'd lost the gamble, he'd eluded me this time for ever and now I wanted to go home. But I felt calm. I didn't care any more. I'd had my Arab experience. As I looked around me, up at the tall slow trees, I knew I'd be back another time, for different reasons.

The car was there and they walked slowly with me to it. I opened the front passenger door and the old woman rapped her knuckles on the window of the back seat and pointed.

I shrugged. "It's OK."

Ramazan, who had just woken up, slumped over the steering wheel. He looked up from his dropped head like a yoked animal. The old woman kept rapping; she seemed upset. Ramazan pointed to the back seat. I got out and went in the back. I didn't understand, but I wanted to go. I rolled down the back window and looked for a moment at the house and the yard beyond, the three goats, their black heads, the shimmering yellow-green weeds of the plain field. It was as shabby as my grandmother's house in Wisconsin, the land as old. I was sad over how many different lives there were and we only got once.

*

Ramazan explained with the guidebook. "Rich," he said and he looked at me, nodding his head. He said the word again, repeating to memorise. I shook my head. He persisted. The wind tore through the open windows. My mother had always told me we were royalty over here. I laughed out loud. Twenty-two Station Street was a good house, but it wasn't royal anywhere in the world. The car stopped: I didn't know why. There was a small stand of dusty olive trees by the side of the road. Ramazan got out and I heard him pee on the dry leaves. Below him was an old stone amphitheatre. I came up behind him, toppled him, and we lay there on the cool stone, toying. I hurt my back once on a eucalyptus button.

"Greco-Roman," he said, pointing to the stage below. It was a small, perfectly tiered circle. There was life there once.

"Arabs have everything, huh?"

"No, Egyptians." He tapped his chest. "We have got pyramids. Antiquities. History." He made a sound by letting air out of his mouth.

When I put my underwear on again, the good pair, drops of blood trickled to the cotton, staining like a watercolour. I found the last scrap of paper from my wallet, on which the woman with the parrot had written that I was looking for my father who might be in Alexandria and that I hadn't seen him for seventeen years. I gave it to Ramazan. He spent a long time reading it.

In the car his face took on a new cast and he lost the plot of his smile. His hands stayed on the wheel, not playful any more. I showed him the word in the book that means airport. I made wing motions with my arms, pointed at myself – "Me, America." We drove a long time keeping the silence and arrived in Cairo. On the way to the airport, he drove through a district of mansions on the Nile. They had domed towers, minarets, columns and mosaics, like mosques. They looked a thousand years old, or older. This was the royalty of Egypt.

"Heliopolis," he said. He stopped before one mansion and pointed. "Omar Sharif."

At the airport, he came into the terminal with me. I studied the English television screen. There was a flight in the evening at eight o'clock. It was only three. He took my hand and I followed him to a phone booth. He was carrying my pack again and it felt easy to let him. It was a modern phone booth. He lifted a book, paged through, found a spot and showed me. I remembered from his hand that Arabic scans from right to left.

His hand brailled over the whole page. "Atassi," he said. "Atassi. Atassi. Atassi."

I smiled and shook my head. It was too late for that. I wanted to go home. I sat on his lap. I didn't want to close the book over a page of Atassis. He ripped the page out, folded it up, put it in my backpack, zipped the zipper. We had time to eat. He drove me to a neighbourhood of low two-storey tenement buildings. Children played in the bare street. The restaurant was small and underground, and we sat cross-legged on the floor. A short-stemmed pink rose leaned in a tin can on our table. Two of the petals, cleft in the centre, had fallen to the cloth. Light slanted into the room from back and front. Ramazan ordered in Arabic and I sat low against a pillow. We looked at each other and sometimes smiled, sometimes didn't; we had stopped trying to use words. The food began to come and set our clock. Olives and new cheese, then kibbe, then my father's layered pancake with a different butter and burnt sugar. He'd always talked about the Bedouin food, about sleeping outside with them as a boy, the open fires in the morning. The pancake tasted of honey and deep caramel and rose water. I handed Ramazan a pencil and paper for the name. He drew and whispered: "Fatir."

Then we used the guidebook. He pointed to his chest and showed me the word 'poor'. I smiled a little, embarrassed for him. He didn't have to ask me. I'd already decided to give him all the money I had and save only twenty dollars for the bus home from the airport. He pointed to himself again, made wing motions and said, in an accent I'd never heard, "America." He pointed to me and I smiled. I gave him my address, and he put it in the little bag he had around his neck where he kept money, and clasped it shut. He took my left hand and banded a cleft rose petal over my third finger. I knew before looking in the book. "Marrying," he said. I got up to leave. He's so young, I was thinking.

It was still light when we walked outside. I wanted to buy a souvenir. We had more than an hour. With the guidebook I showed him the word for bazaar and I shrugged. We walked into a district of close streets and corners, brown buildings and smells of burning meat. We came to a square filled with market stands and around the sides were the neon-lit fronts of casinos. He pulled me over to the edge of the square, where there was a tiled drinking fountain and a man standing with a camera draped in black cloth and a camel tied to a palm. He spoke and seemed to be asking if I wanted to have my picture taken with the camel.

We surveyed the stands of the bazaar. From a dusty market table, we picked out an everyday Turkish coffee pot, a little one. I wanted to open the jar of what my father had liked. When the woman had given it to me, I thought I'd save it for my father and give it to him as a present the first time I saw him, if I ever found him and we met again. But I didn't want to wait. I'd waited and saved enough for him. The lid stuck. I gave it to Ramazan. He held it against his belly, straining, and again I thought, he's young, and then it was open. It was a rich distilled paste that tasted of almonds and honey. We ate it with our fingers as we walked past fabric bolts and animals that licked our hands. We finished the whole jar. I turned my back for a moment and he bought me a dress. I had been staring at a painted wooden cut-out of a bride and groom propped outside a casino called the Monte Carlo. The heads were open circles for people to stand in and have their picture taken. BE THE BRIDE, it said.

In the airport I bought a snowball paperweight that showed a scene with camels and tents in the desert. Ramazan paid for it. He'd paid for the coffee pot, for dinner, for the dress, and he'd tried to pay for the wedding photographs. We passed a bar called the Ramadan Room, where an orchestrated version of 'Home of the Brave' was playing. At the departure gate I tried to give him my money. I had two hundred and ten dollars in cash. I wanted to give him all of it. He wouldn't take it. I pushed the crinkled bills into his pockets. His mouth got hard; his chin made a clean line; he took it all, balled it, jammed it down in my pack.

At the metal security bar we drank a long goodbye kiss. His articulate hands moved around my face as if fashioning an imaginary veil there.

"Goodbye," I said. I knew absolutely that I would never see him again.

He said words I didn't understand but I made out Allah. Everything in his language had to do with God.

from

The American Woman in the Chinese Hat

Carole Maso

Carole Maso is the author of the novels *Ghost Dance*, *The Art Lover*, *AVA*, *The American Woman in the Chinese Hat* and *Aureole*. She teaches at Brown University.

I go to Arles by train. Van Gogh walked there one hundred years ago and that is good enough for me. On the train I write her letters I won't send. I sit in a cage with five German men who look out at the sea and then to me. I don't know what anything means. I never used to look for meaning, but now I feel that need. I realise I am already braced for the next disaster.

I have called in advance and reserved a room in a hotel on 'La Place du Docteur Pomme'. I suppose I have come to try to get well. No weeping women here, I think, putting away the letters I have begun to her.

I'm the last one off the train. A young woman looks at me and immediately begins to cry. "What is it?" I ask.

"You are the last person on the train," she says in French. "He is not coming."

"Perhaps he will be on the train tomorrow," I say.

"*Non.*" She cries and cries. "He has said that if he was not on this train it would mean he is not coming, never coming."

I think to myself this is such a sad life.

We decide to go to a café together. She orders an *eau minérale*. It turns out he is her first lover, a painter she had been modelling for. The man is *Anglais* and she has learned some English from him. She says that her heart is breaking.

I tell her the heart is more fragile than fruit. It can't be handled tenderly enough.

She smiles. "You are very kind," she says.

She was born in the Camargue. She is seventeen. One could easily understand the desire to paint her – the thick dark hair, the full breasts and hips. She hopes one day to model in Paris. It is her dream. "I will show you the town," she decides.

Caesar made Arles a Roman colony, and the whole town seems like a vast museum. It is hers and she walks through it, majestic and damaged. A statue. We go to the cloisters, the amphitheatre, the *arènes*. At the *arènes* she says, "They have bullfights here. Spanish music plays. Sometimes I can smell blood." We walk along the Rhone.

At dinner we sit at the forum, a huge open square bordered by plane trees. Small white lights are strung up everywhere. It's still hot. A French man with a guitar sings a Simon and Garfunkel song, "I swear I was so lonely that I took some comfort there." It's an odd thing to hear.

She talks more about the man. "He is a very great painter, I think," she says. But it makes her sad to say much more. "Tell me something else," I say. She tells me she rode wild horses as a girl. "The horses are born brown," she says, "and they turn white when they are grown. They are very beautiful. *Sauvage.* There are great pink and orange birds there," she says. "My father grows rice. You would like it. Maybe some day we could go."

Il fait chaud. She has already said she is most comfortable without clothes.

"I must go," I say, "to the Place du Docteur Pomme. But tomorrow."

For a long time the next morning I watch the concierge feeding birds. Her outstretched fingers scatter crumbs. Every gesture in this light feels enormous, archetypal. I walk to the woman's house. Her name is Dominique. "*Bonjour*, Catherine." We drink *café* on a terrace in bright light. "*Il fait trop chaud*," she says.

She tells me last night she cried herself to sleep.

168

"How did it happen, with the man?"

"*Un moment.*" She goes into the house for a minute. "I was wearing this." She shows me a bright blue silk robe. "He bought it for me. All the way from China. He began to paint, but he did not like my pose. He said to try putting my hand here," and she put it between her breasts. "Move in here," he said, and she put her hand on her thigh. Then between her legs. "He asked me to make it look like I was touching myself there. He said if I wanted I could touch myself. He kissed me. I had never made love before. He knew this and kissed me just slightly. Barely, barely brushing my lips. *Comme ça.*" And she shows me. "It was like that that he kissed me at first. Later he would bruise my lips, the way he would kiss me.

"We went back to the pose. My hand here."

"Did you like that?"

"I liked it most when he was watching and I was thinking of that gentle kiss, *oui.* Later it was different. I longed for the time when there was only that smallest of kisses."

We go for a walk. I take her to my rented room on La Place du Docteur Pomme.

"Once he had me pose with another woman. She was like the English are. Like you. At first I was jealous of her. He was very wise. He saw this. He told me to touch her neck gently like the kiss had been. He said it must seem relaxed, natural. We became friends, the fair woman and me. I grew to like her very much. She was twenty-eight, older. She said she had been modelling for eight years. In Paris. That often afterwards she made love with them. But I never felt as happy as when I was touching her neck, gazing into her face in our pose."

"Where is she now?"

"She was about to marry. She lived with a painter in Paris.

169

One day I will go to Paris.

"Have you ever modelled?"

"No. *Je suis ecrivaine.*"

"*Vraiment?* What do you write?"

"Stories about love and then love taken away."

"They are sad, then?"

"Yes. They are sad stories."

"I love sad stories. Stories that make me cry. I don't know why." She thought of the painter. His name was Nigel. "You know then about sadness?"

"I am twenty-eight. I am the same age as the woman whose neck you touched. It is old enough to know a great deal about sadness."

"You are more beautiful than that woman. Don't be sad now."

My hair is pinned up. She dares to touch my neck. She brushes my lips with her mouth again. "I know nothing," she whispers, "except that Nigel had me touch her neck, touch myself and then put my finger to her lips. That is all."

"Like this?"

"*Oui.* I did it for the painting. It was my work. But I could never forget after that. Even though I felt *honte.*"

"What is that?"

"*Ce n'est pas bon.* It's hard to explain." She puts her dark finger to my lips. We hold the pose a long time.

I take each finger gently, gently into my mouth and she lets out a small sigh.

"*Un petit goût,*" I say. She nods. She is sweet like the ripe melons of Cavillon. "*Tiens.*"

"*Un petit goût, s'il te plaît.*" Her robe falls open. Her dark body gives off an extraordinary light. She seems to glisten.

She touches my neck again. She applies just the slightest

pressure. Her touch tells me she wants more. She wants my mouth on her breasts. I touch her round belly. She nods. She wants my mouth to descend to that triangle, it's luxurious, dark. And she too needs a small taste. She grows. She grows wild. She turns from a brown horse into a white one. I pull her magnificent mane, press her between her thighs. Ride into light.

"Dominique."

Every tree bears fruit here. All afternoon we eat plums, figs. "It's my birthday," she says.

I sing her the birthday song, off-key. She laughs. "You are so lovely," I say. She is eighteen.

I run my wrists under cool water in the terrible heat of the room.

In the night she says, "Perhaps you will write a story about me. It will be a little sad this story – but mostly no."

Something opens that cannot be closed. Heat opens us further. Bees. There's an incredible lushness. "You are so delicious," I say.

"*Et toi!*" I can scarcely believe what ripens in me.

*

Overnight the Sirocco had come driving the Sahara into France, into our throats and onto the hoods of the cars of Vence. I write her name – Elena – in the sand. The umbrellas at La Regence fly off their axis. I am happy to be back in this town I have begun to memorise. Because to know the pattern in the door or the design of stones in the street or the gratings and railings in every kind of light helps, a little.

She says there is someone else, and suddenly everything is sand.

I step into the garden of the Hotel de Provence and order a Pernod. I can still smell the woman from Arles in my hair, on my skin. I'm alone here; no one else in the garden and I like that.

"It's my birthday," she whispers in my ear. "Do this for me. Don't move much or someone will see. Shh – pretend you are modelling. Now move your hand to your breast. Now move your hand again. I'll be watching you," she says. "I'll be touching your neck." I open my legs, moving only slightly. The tip of my finger on the tip of my clitoris.

I wonder if someone upstairs parting the curtain watches this trembling woman as she touches herself in the *jardin* of the Hotel de Provence. I have fantasised too precisely. A man appears out of nowhere. He walks through arbours, under trellises.

"*Excuses-moi,*" he says, "but I have to know, what is that scent? It is so familiar to me."

"*Je ne comprends pas,*" I say.

The wind picks up suddenly. The wind stirs up everything. There's sand in my eyes. I hear the voice of an old woman in the next villa shouting in English, "We'll all be blown to bits."

"*Ton parfum,*" he says. "*Qu'est-ce que c'est?*" He asks to sit. I nod.

"I ask because I am in the business of perfume. And it is making me crazy – the name for that scent."

"*La Jeune Arlésienne,*" I say.

from
Frontiers of Heaven

Stanley Stewart

Stanley Stewart was born in Ireland, grew up in Canada and lives in London. He is the author of *Old Serpent Nile* and *Frontiers of Heaven*, and is also a regular contributor to *The Sunday Times*, the *Daily Telegraph* and the *Sunday Telegraph*.

Outside the east gate of the city walls, in a narrow park between the ramparts and a canal, opera was performed each evening in an atmosphere reminiscent of Elizabethan theatre. Lanterns hung in the trees and the audience, mainly old people, sat on low benches before a makeshift stage. The men waggled their fans and pulled their trousers above their knees to reveal hairless legs. The old women smoked cigars stuck upright into clay pipes. Everyone sipped jars of tea in which the leaves floated like seaweed. It was a jolly social occasion for which the opera offered a stirring backdrop. Fu Wen and I joined the crowds standing around the periphery with their bicycles.

The performance was stylised, almost ritualistic. The characters, swathed in layers of tawdry silks, tottered across the plank stage on block sandals, nodding beneath tiered headgear. Long pheasant-tail plumes bobbed in their wake. Their faces were garish masks of make-up. Every detail conveyed meaning. Red cheeks indicated loyalty, white suggested cunning. A gesture conjured armies. Another carried the action from the battlefield to the palace. When the actors took to imaginary horses, their cavalry status was declared with pretty feathery whips. Long journeys were described by walking in circles.

The usual conspiracies of theatrical illusion seemed unimportant here. The orchestra – five old men in their vests – sat down stage, sawing away on two-stringed viols and clashing tinny cymbals like extras who had forgotten their costumes. Between acts the singers strolled through the crowds making assignations. Characters who had died in the preceding act turned up in the interval, in full costume, selling ice lollies. On stage their children, toddlers in crotchless pants, got under the feet of invading armies. Boredom was rife among the spear-carriers, who spent their time mouthing comments to friends in the audience. One fell asleep against a pillar and had to be woken to be slain in battle.

With our heads inclined together, Fu Wen told me the story as it unfolded. The cacophonous music, the garish faces, the trailing gowns, were reduced to something intimate between us. She rested her hand on my bicycle and told me of empires falling.

When it was over we drifted away through the park following the line of the walls toward the south gate. Along the empty paths, away from the crowds, Fu Wen grew animated. She sang scraps of opera. She laughed. She asked about my journey and when I told her about the Yangtze, she brimmed over with questions. Her eagerness was a kind of yearning. Yesterday, I marvelled, I had not even met this woman who now filled the evening. Through the dark trees I could see the lighted road on the other side of the canal where, with its bicycles and scooter trucks and roadside stalls, life appeared to be going on as before.

I rode her home, down a long avenue tunnelling beneath plane trees into the southern suburbs. It was unlit except for the red lanterns of roadside stalls. Occasionally cars passed, their head-lights illuminating the road, the trees, the dark shopfronts, like searchlights.

At a corner she stopped. Her house was nearby. She did not want me to see her to the door. We stood straddling our bicycles in the middle of the dark lane.

"Can I see you tomorrow?" I asked.

She thought for a moment. "In the afternoon," she said.

We tried to think where we could meet. Her need for discretion, her fear of gossip, limited the choices. She did not want to meet at the Institute.

"The Great Mosque," I said at last. "Two o'clock?"

She nodded. I leaned into the shadows and kissed her goodnight, then she turned and cycled away. In the long avenue I was grateful for the navigation lights of the roadside stalls. I would hardly have known the way. Xi'an and China suddenly seemed so different.

*

In the morning the road to the Terracotta Army was fretted with sunlight. I had hardly slept, and set off early, happy for the distractions of an expedition to the beginnings of China, to the tomb of the man who built the Great Wall. A puncture delayed me briefly on the outskirts of town but a bicycle repair man, working from a cardboard box beneath a tree, fixed it for tuppence, throwing in a free service. I rode through a dusty landscape of haystacks and pomegranate orchards. Pink blossoms drifted in the lanes and the road was stained with fruit.

For centuries the large earth mound which marked the tomb of Qin Shiuhuang had attracted no more attention than the many other tumuli which littered the plains around Xi'an. Then in 1974 a farmer, digging a well in the corner of his orchard, struck something hard with his spade. When he cleared the loose earth he found not a rock but a clay head, the first glimpse of what was to be the most astonishing archaeological discovery of the century.

Excavation revealed thousands of life-sized terracotta soldiers, arrayed in battle formation, complete with horses and chariots, an honour guard for the dead emperor. After twenty years of digging there is still no end in sight. The 6000 soldiers uncovered thus far may represent only a small fraction of the total army. Work has yet to begin on the tomb itself. The Chinese, typically, are taking the long view.

Ancient records describe the tomb of Qin Shiuhuang as a fabulous underground landscape. The ceilings were said to be inlaid with pearls to simulate the night sky. Trees were carved from precious stones. Gold and silver birds flitted among their leaves while rivers of mercury flowed beneath them. Historians were apt to dismiss these fantastical accounts, until the discovery of the Terracotta Army. Its scale suddenly makes anything possible.

The occupant of this extraordinary mausoleum ruled China for a mere fifteen years. The dynasty he founded did not survive his death. Yet his importance is undisputed. He was called the First Emperor. When he came to the throne in 221 BC he found a group of warring states. When he died in 207, he left behind a single nation, China, a corruption of the dynastic name Qin. He was a tyrant on the grand scale. He not only burnt books, he had their authors buried alive. He executed whole families for the crimes committed by one of their members. He conscripted thousands of workers for his endless building schemes and when they were disloyal enough to die on the job, he used their bodies as land-fill. Among his many projects was the construction of the Great Wall.

The army that was to protect him against the terrors of the underworld is now sheltered by an arena which protects it from the rain. Inside the soldiers stand in long trenches, rank upon orderly rank, a composed and confident company. Each statue is an individual portrait; of the 6000, no two are alike.

They seem pleased at their resurrection, as if they had

returned from a long and arduous campaign and were now basking, a little smugly, in the admiration of the crowds who turn out to greet them. Nothing lends them a sense of verismo so much as their duplicity, the familiar military conspiracy to hide the more grisly aspects of their victories. Like a real returning army, they present their best face to the world: the orderly ranks, the neat Edwardian beards, the untroubled brows, the faint smiles. These are, however, reconstructions. At the rear of the trenches, beneath canvas shrouds, lies a less picturesque reality. Here the figures are still encased in the earth. Heads, limbs, torsos, are jumbled together like broken china, the carnage of a bombed regiment, kept neatly out of sight of the admiring crowds.

*

I had lunch near the hot springs of Hua Qing, where generations of emperors built elegant pavilions and bathhouses. The Tang emperor Gao Zong spent so much time here dallying with his concubine, the fabled beauty Yang Guifei, that his ministers were obliged to have her assassinated in order to get him to concentrate on affairs of state. Hua Qing is full of such charming love stories.

After lunch I went for a bath in a local bathhouse that was like a cross between a boxer's gym and a cave. An attendant with a towel round his neck gave me a locker and I disrobed. Along a corridor I found naked Chinese men floundering through the steam. Whatever their age they seemed to have the bodies of adolescents, as smooth and slippery as seals. When I lowered myself into one of the two pools of creamy green water, its occupants fell silent then discreetly got out and climbed into the other. Later in the changing room, I looked round to find them gazing at me through a doorway, their faces twitching with curiosity.

I bullied my way onto a bus back to Xi'an, riding on the roof with my bicycle amid sacks of flour. In town I hurried to the Great Mosque, hidden in the winding lanes of the Muslim quarter. You turn a blind corner and fall into a garden of Chinese arches and pavilions, overblown flowers and old men with caged crickets. In its journey from the west Islam has travelled lightly, and the mosque has taken the form of a Chinese temple.

I could not find her at first, and was surprised at the strength of my dismay when I thought she had not come. But when I went back to the main gate there she was, waiting with her red bicycle, and all was suddenly well with the world again.

Fu Wen had not been to the Great Mosque before, and along the flagstone paths and through the grey-tiled pavilions she was suddenly the stranger and I the guide. I pointed out the Arabic inscriptions trailing like vines above a lintel. I explained about the cluster of shoes left outside the doors, the muezzin, the prayers which leaked into the daylight, and the traders who had come from Arabia and Persia more than a thousand years ago. I went on at such nervous length that she assumed I was a Muslim, and asked why I was not going to prayers.

In a small court off the main gardens, where potted ferns trailed over an empty fountain and birds gossiped in the rafters, we sat all afternoon talking, until the dark came. Among the frangipanis shedding their petals and the warnings of the muezzin, we were falling towards one another.

When the evening prayers were over the old men in their white caps drifted through the gardens to the communion of stone benches. Fu Wen buried her hand in mine.

"How long will you stay here?" she asked.

In my pocket I had a train ticket for the following day. I had already mentally discarded it.

"A week," I said. I had no idea.

"Where will you go then?"

"To Lanzhou. And then to Gansu."

At the base of her throat the small indentation, like a thumb-mark, trembled with her pulse. Her lips moved. Something unspoken waited inside her mouth.

"Come with me," I said. "Come to Tulufan. Come to Wulumuchi. Come to Kashi. I will meet you there. When can you come?"

She looked at me with narrowing eyes as if across a glare of distance.

"It is not possible," she said.

I put my lips to the little spoon of skin, the soft pulse. She tilted her head back against a pillar, an equine arching. Her skin was buttery and smelt of almonds.

In the twilight the old men's pet crickets were singing their hearts out. They sang of love, the males and females serenading one another across the darkening gardens from their little wicker cages. Their duets could last for hours. In protracted litanies of offerings and responses, they were trying to identify and assess one another. If one of them departed from the melody by as little as a fourth of a tone, the exchange was abandoned, to be taken up again later with another. It was a quest for compatibility, the wisdom of crickets.

*

Her grandfather had been a landowner. It was not a large estate, a few orchards and small-holdings let to farmers on the edge of

Xi'an, but it was to lie like a shadow across three generations of the family. In the land reforms after the revolution it was taken under state control as part of a communal farm. Her grandfather was fortunate. Many landowners, denounced by their tenants, were executed by revolutionary tribunals. He was simply stripped of his possessions. His tenants had been quite fond of him.

Her grandfather spent his remaining years ill and embittered. He complained that no one really cared for the land. They planted their crops and harvested them 'like factory workers', he would say, with scant regard for the unproductive, the merely decorative. For him the land had a spiritual dimension. Ancestor worship is part of Chinese religious tradition, and the loss of the family estates was akin to the desecration of their graves. A few years after land reform the committee decided to chop down the orchards. They had been planted by his great-grandfather. The committee said the trees were past their best.

"Perhaps they were," Fu Wen said. "But he could never reconcile himself. He went in the evenings and sat on the stumps. My father had to go each night and fetch him home. He died of a broken heart."

In the new classless China, everyone was strictly categorised according to class background. It appeared on one's identity papers after name and date of birth. The children of peasants found themselves first in line for jobs, housing, education while those with a bourgeois background were often denied preferment. The Party believed in a bloodline concept of guilt which held that the descendants of 'bad elements' like landlords must carry the continuing stigma of their forbears' guilt. It was official policy until 1978.

When the mania of the Cultural Revolution began in the

summer of 1966, her parents were students. In that fateful spring her father had the misfortune to come top of his class. Her mother's crime was potentially more serious. She wanted to be a writer, and had already had poetry and stories published in the local newspaper. These were to mark her out for special ridicule.

In the autumn term, study was abandoned in favour of rallies, public criticism and confessions. Teachers were denounced by their students and paraded through the streets in dunces' caps. In a particularly gruesome episode one of her father's tutors was paralysed for life when he was beaten up by the Red Guards for lack of zeal in his own self-criticism. Because he took no part in these persecutions Fu Wen's father immediately fell under suspicion. His good grades marked him out as an 'élitist', addicted to competition. Meanwhile, at public rallies where the unrepentant were beaten, her mother was forced to denounce her own writing as bourgeois and counter-revolutionary.

In the midst of this madness they had married, hoping perhaps to recapture a private world beyond the grasp of public hysteria. It was a vain hope. In early 1968 they were sent to the countryside 'to learn from the peasants'. They were part of one of the greatest movements of population in history. Almost 17 million people were sent into internal exile, one in ten of the urban population. The peasants, regrettably, were not consulted and found themselves suddenly playing host to train-loads of weedy intellectuals who knew nothing about hardship and less about farming.

Though Fu Wen seemed a modern metropolitan woman, she had grown up in the country amongst mud and cabbages. She was born on a communal farm in a remote part of Gansu province, almost 700 miles to the west of Xi'an. At the time the

183

family was living in half of a one-roomed house, a curtain dividing their living space from that of the village family who, until their arrival, had had the whole room to themselves. As the years passed, while they swilled out the pigs, ploughed the fields, and waited on the weather, her parents were trying to find a way back to Xi'an, to some shadow of their former lives. Long after the Cultural Revolution had subsided, its victims, in their millions, were still stranded in their places of exile all over China, unable to find their way through the labyrinth of permits, job searches and housing queues that would take them home. Eighteen years after their departure, Fu Wen's family returned home to Xi'an.

With the help of her former tutors, Fu Wen's mother secured a post as a primary school teacher. Her father, who had been one of the brightest mathematical minds of his academic year, found a job as accountancy clerk in a shoe factory. They were assigned a flat in the southern suburbs. It stood on land that had once been part of her grandfather's orchards.

*

The years of zealotry had left the habit of protecting oneself against criticism, personal as much as political. Reputations were guarded like fortunes. Fu Wen was terrified of gossip.

I never went to the Institute again. Fu Wen telephoned me to arrange our assignations. We spent the afternoons in my hotel room, which we reached by the back stairs. When we hired a car to go out of town to visit the western tombs, she wanted to check first that the driver was not someone she knew. In the streets we found our steps turning to the empty avenues atop the city walls. The secrecy irritated me but for Fu Wen I think it became part of the excitement. In a life of constraints, the illicit flexes powerful muscles.

In the dwindling hours we had together, Fu Wen fussed over me, worried that I might become ill, that I would be lonely, that people would take advantage of me. She became maternal, arriving with packets of green tea and home-made dumplings. I was the hardened traveller, crossing half of Asia, and she grew tearful about my vulnerabilities. I admired her intelligence and her strength. She worried how I would cope.

In the afternoons in the hotel room with the curtains drawn we retreated into a world of our own creation, a landscape of limbs, a neutral territory with only two citizens, their divided loyalties happily disguised.

The hotel was opposite the railway station. The whistle of the trains, the shouts of the guards, the muffled announcement of destinations, crept into our world almost unnoticed. Later when we stepped outside into the crowds hurrying through the dusk we seemed to be infected with their collective anxiety about arrivals and departures. The people and the traffic, pressing homeward, broke the delightful sense of suspension in which we had passed the afternoon. Jogged into motion again, I felt us moving apart as if we were now on different trains.

In the crowded cafés of the Jiefang Market where we went for dinner, the sense of distance after the intimacies of the afternoon seemed unbearable. I rode her home along Chang'an Lu beneath the dark arches of the plane trees. Saying goodbye in the lane broke my heart every evening. When she cycled away into the darkness I longed to call after her, to call across the widening frontiers.

*

"It is a dream," she said. "Don't confuse this with real life."

We were on top of the city walls. We came here often to be alone. I was ripping up my notebooks to make paper aeroplanes which we launched from these empty heights into courtyards and back lanes, unobserved. Sheltering in the old pavilions, among the starlings and the litter of lovers, I realised we were hiding like truants, hiding from China. I flew a folded Concorde to her.

"I am twenty-eight," she said, jumping up to catch the paper glider. "All my school friends are married and have children. My parents are worried about me. They want to see me settled."

"What do you want?" I asked.

"I want to find a life where I can be happy." She sounded like a traveller turning homeward, that odd mix of resignation and anticipation. "We cannot be happy together. Only briefly, now." I felt like a child, standing there with my paper aeroplanes. I knew what she was saying, but I did not want to listen to it.

"Why should I give you my life?" she said. "You would not know what to do with it."

"I want to go home," I said.

We took a taxi to the hotel.

Let's Go

Emily Perkins

Emily Perkins was born in Christchurch, New Zealand, in 1970 and grew up in Auckland and Wellington. She attended the New Zealand Drama School/Te Kura Toi Whakaari o Aotearoa, and currently lives and works in London. She is the author of *Not Her Real Name* and *Leave Before You Go*, published by Picador.

L et's go to Roxy, we say. Let's go to FX.

I try to learn some of the language, but don't get beyond 'diky', which means thanks. Informal. Casual. Friendly. The formal way is 'dekuji vam', but it's easier not to bother with the distinction. I find myself lost, wandering up and down a block looking for the Globe Café (I am two crucial streets away from it, but I don't know this). I stop people and ask, Do you speak English? and they shake their heads and smile. Diky, I call after them, diky, diky. Diky for nothing!

We go to Roxy, we go to FX.

Grunge, announces Hal, hit Prague like a soggy mattress.

He's right. It looks like it's here to stay, in every bar and café we visit. Americans, Americans. Thousands of dollars but they dress as if they're slumming it.

We stand outside the theatres and study the black & white photographs. Scenes from Beckett, Anouilh, Ionesco. Seriousness. Raised fists. Absurdity. We laugh.

We come across a candles-and-flowers shrine commemorating the Velvet Revolution. There are poems which we cannot read. Some tourists wander up and stand behind us, at a deferential distance. We don't speak until they are gone. We want them to believe what we briefly believe, that this is our memorial, our pain, our revolution. They back away with the hush of the guilty. We look at each other and we laugh. Hal reads a poem out loud in nonsensical Czech phonetics and we laugh again.

We're hungover at Segafredo and I'm cross because they don't have hangover food. I order a hot chocolate without cream.

The waitress doesn't understand me.

Without cream, I say. No cream.

She looks at Hal for help. He finds me embarrassing.

No cream, I say louder. I don't want any cream with the hot chocolate.

She frowns.

Cream? I don't want any?

I mime pouring cream out of a jug. Thick, I mutter.

Her face is blank. She tells me, It does not come with cream.

I make a mental note of this, for next time.

We go to Roxy, we go to Globe, we go to FX.

Look! says Hal. Poetry readings!

We get a cab to FX for the Saturday night poetry reading. The cab driver has a more explicit collection of pornographic pictures than most. I think about what might be in his car boot. He has a high colour and when someone cuts him out at the lights I think I see specks of foam in the corner of his mouth. His moustache makes it hard to be certain. I worry about apoplexy, and how hard it would be to gain control of the car if he were to clutch at his chest and then collapse suddenly around the steering wheel, inert.

We sit in the big armchairs at the back of FX. Some very beautiful women are there. They are all Czech, which is unusual. A – that they're beautiful (no tan stockings encasing ham-like thighs, no tasselled suede pirate boots, no lurid artificial blush applied over undemure cheeks). B – that they are here in FX, which like every other place we go to is usually inhabited by young people from everywhere in the world except Eastern Europe.

Their eyebrows are plucked excruciatingly thin and without exception they have those fashionably swollen big lips. Hal says there must be a special machine in the girls' loos – press a button and a boxing glove pops out and hits you to create that perfect punched-in-the-mouth look. He mimes being hit by it, his head jerking back in a whip-lash movement. Again! I say, clapping my hands together, Again!

The beautiful women drift in and out, past our chairs, talking intently to each other in low voices. Sheets of paper – their poems! – dangle casually from their fingertips.

Czech chicks, murmurs Hal longingly.

Learn the language, I suggest. That'd be a start.

Diky, he says, morose.

Actually I think the language barrier is no bad thing. It provides a lot of scope for meaningful looks. But it does mean that what we understand by a 'poetry reading' is not what the Czechs understand by one – after much quiet and tender-sounding talk between themselves and passing around of the pieces of paper, they stand up and flowingly, waifishly, leave.

We go to Roxy, we go to Roxy.

Hal dances. I don't, won't, can't. The vodka is cheap. It works out, per plastic cup, at 90p. Or a buck and a quarter. Or two dollars fifty. In any currency, it's a cheap shot. Ha ha. Later, we hear that there is some poisoned Polish vodka floating around the city. It was transported from Kracow in rusty vats. More than seven shots a night, the papers say, could kill a grown man. Even so, we do not die.

The receptionist at the hotel says, There is a message for you. We're excited – a message? Who could it be from? Perhaps it is from our friend Louis who is running a bagel factory somewhere outside the city. Perhaps it is news from home, except that nobody knows where we are. Maybe, I think, it could be from the German boy I gave my number to in Chapeau Rouge last night.

But – unhappy travellers! – the message is from the hotel management. We have chipped a corner off the wooden tag attached to our room key.

You have broken this, the message says, and it was new last week. You must replace it.

We are bewildered. I hand over some kroner.

Now? I ask, unsure what to do.

As you wish, the receptionist says, taking my money and giving me a receipt which she first stamps three times.

Sorry about that, we say, and we laugh.

Prague is not a good place to be vegetarian. We go to dinner and order three or four different kinds of meat, which all arrive on the same plate but cooked in different ways. It is a flesh-fest. Hal pretends to adore it but even he is unable to finish the last piece of liver. Vegetables, we say. We want vegetables. When they come they are recently thawed diced things from out of a packet: carrot, sweetcorn, peas. Vodka, we say. We want vodka. Ha ha ha.

Apparently, there are a number of things I do which infuriate Hal. I embarrass him in cafés (the hot chocolate incident); I embarrass him in bars (the German boy incident). I talk too loudly in the street and I can be 'pretentious'. Pretentious, moi? Hal's objections surprise me. We are like an old married couple. He says 'huh' too often (he claims to be unaware of this) and his jaw clicks when he eats. Or is that my father? I can't be sure.

It's too hot in our hotel! The radiators are up full blast. Gusts of warm air chase us down the halls. Our room is a little heat pit. I wake up with gunky eyes and burning sinuses.

The hotel is large. We suspect that there are no other guests. Every now and then – sometimes very early in the morning – we hear the distant whine of a vacuum cleaner on another floor. Who are they vacuuming for? They never vacuum for us. We lie on our beds, stifling in the thick air, rubbing at our sticky eyes. The windows do not open. I decide it is sinister that the windows do not open. After the broken key tag situation it is hard for me to trust the hotel staff. Perhaps the room is bugged. They have our passports, after all. Every night I expect to come back to some fresh damage and another bill for repair. A hole punched in the wall, possibly a broken chair. The suffocating heat does not diminish my unease.

Dear Alicia, I write on a postcard to my sister, We are having a wonderful time in Prague and looking after our hotel room very well. The Czech hospitality is marvellous.

I hand it to the receptionist to post. I smile at her. Diky, post, please, I say. You post?, nodding – Stamp? Diky.

Don't shout, hisses Hal from behind me. You'll ruin everything. You post, I say, please, diky, read it, you silly slav cow, diky.

We make a new friend at the Globe. His name is Dick and he's American. A New Yorker, he tells us, but will later under the influence of vodka admit he is from 'Joisey'. Dick and Hal play backgammon while I write letters I will never send, and drink tumblerfuls of red wine, and listen. Dick's just been in Vietnam.

Oh yeah, he says, it was beautiful. Like going back in time, man. This incredible French architecture, women in long silk pants. Unbelievably cheap, you know, everything. He snickers. And I mean everything.

Hal snickers too. I look at the rain on the Globe's windows and try to imagine Saigon.

We take Dick back to our hotel, where I get changed, and on to the Whale Bar. Vodka, vodka, we cry. Dick pays for everything in American money. In Vietnam, he tells us, he decided to become a dong millionaire. He exchanged however many hundred US dollars into Vietnamese dong, until he had a suitcase filled with great bricks of money. He kept the million dong locked in this suitcase in his hotel room for a week, not touching it. Then he got crazy on Long Island Iced Tea one night after this little Spanish senorita he'd been going with left town. He gambled every last bit of the money away, ha ha ha, playing poker and twenty-one.

I challenge him to a game of twenty-one, feeling lucky because it's my age and besides I'm rather good at it, but Hal cuts in and says I'm not allowed. Dick and Hal both smile at me, like older brothers, like members of the same team. What can I do?

Czech chicks! Czech chicks! Hal is getting desperate. It is difficult for him, travelling with me in tow. He accuses me of sabotaging all his flirtatious encounters. I can't help it. Mostly I try not to, but sometimes when he goes to the bathroom I look at the girl he's been eyeing up and I give her the evils. I'm only protecting him from himself, after all. Things got nasty once, in Warsaw. Hal fell in with a bad crowd, turpentine, death metal, etcetera, and I had to bail him out. This short Polack girl glommed onto us and wouldn't leave our hotel. Crying, carrying on. Baby, she kept saying, baby. Either it was the only English she knew or it was a serious accusation. Some meat-faced guy who said he was her brother turned up on the scene, ranting and raving. Hal didn't like the idea of a big Polish wedding so we shoved some cigarettes at them and split town. I'm not ready to leave Prague yet, so Hal will just have to keep himself in hand. Ha ha ha.

Petrin Hill. What a climb! The heels on my boots stick into the earth and I skid on wet leaves. Hal has to drag me up most of the way while Dick strides on ahead. By the time we're at the top my arms are only just still in their sockets. Something awful happens. Hal doubles over outside the observatory. It could be his back problem. Or it could be liver failure. It makes a good photograph. Aaoow, he says, aaoow. I say cheese while Dick clicks the camera. Tears come out of Hal's eyes. I hold his hands. I feel that I should because some nights he sits on the edge of his bed while I sit on the edge of mine and he holds my hands. (Those are the nights I can't breathe or speak, the nights when the world is spinning way too fast and giving me the shakes. Vodka and cigarettes fail to stop these shakes any more but Hal holding my hands sometimes helps.) It doesn't seem the same rule applies to his back pain. Aaoow, aaoow. Poor baby. I make him lie flat on the damp ground and wipe the sweat off his face. I look around for Dick but he's not there. Help, I shout to the passers-by, Au secours! They keep on passing by. Hal pants and whimpers some more. It hurts to watch him. Then Dick reappears with a hip-flask of whisky. Hal drinks some and shuts his eyes and smiles. His whimpering subsides. He gets to his feet and laughs. What a relief! We love Dick! We jump around. We run all over the top of the hill taking photographs of each other. We are a music video.

Franz Kafka was one skinny guy. Kind of good-looking though. Huh, says Hal, you think so?

He thinks I'm shallow. To prove him wrong I buy a copy of *The Trial*. I will read it soon, right after I've finished *Laughable Loves*.

Dick has hours of fun reading the Police Service note on his street map. "Dear friends," he shouts to us in a cod Czech accent as we walk up to meet him outside the usual place, "for the answer to your question, how the crime in Prague differs from the crime in other European cities, it is possible to say: in no way!"

Or, hysterically, in Whale he will tell the barman, "In the number of committed criminal acts counted for 100,000 inhabitants the Czech Republic is in the order after the Netherlands, Germany, Austria and Switzerland. Therefore Prague is a quiet oasis basically."

He has memorised it. Hal groans and wrinkles his nose but I could listen to it over and over again.

Dick also likes to remind us that, "Prague has street prostitutes, too. You can see them in Prelova Street and in a part of Narodni Street. We do not recommend to contact them."

Hal and Dick have left me alone! Meanies. They've gone 'out on the town' and didn't let me go with them. You better not leave the hotel, they said to me. It's not safe for a young girl alone in the big city.

Life is a cabaret, old chum, they sing as they swing down the stairs of the hotel, leaving me standing forlorn in the doorway, calling out, We do not recommend to contact them. We do NOT recommend it.

I go to Whale, I go to Roxy.

At Roxy I am drinking vodka and not dancing. I am wearing tight Lycra and am highly groomed in order to stand out from the babydoll T-shirts, grubby denim and ornamental hairclips around me. I look fantastique. A boy of I guess about seventeen makes eyes at me. I make eyes back. Then I ignore him, kind of cool. He walks past me. He has a nice body. He turns and smiles at me. I smile back. He walks back past me the other way. I laugh into my vodka. He beckons me to come and sit with him and his friends. I saunter over.

Hi, I say.

Hi, they say. One of them lights my cigarette.

Are you having becher? says the one about to go to the bar. They are Czech! This is perfect. It is cultural relations. Foreign affairs. They buy me drinks even though the money I nicked from Hal's secret supply at the hotel would probably pay their rent for a month. They are economics students.

After the revolution, the one who is still making eyes at me explains, we all wanted to be businessmen. Yuppies. They laugh at this, and I laugh too. Now they would all rather be poets. It is more romantic. But they've enrolled in their courses and they must finish them, or their parents would be disappointed. They ask me what I do and I tell them nothing. They are jealous. They are stoned.

This grass, my boyfriend says, is extra strong. Do you know why? It is because of the acid rain that rained down on all the plants after Chernobyl. The acid gets into the dope and makes it extra strong.

I stifle a yawn.

The friends go to dance and leave me alone with my boyfriend. He has a beautiful smile and a slow blink so I kiss him.

That'll show Hick and Dal.

The Hunger Wall. So-called because at the time it was built there was great poverty. Those men who worked on the wall were guaranteed food. Therefore they did not go hungry. Therefore it was a good thing to heave boulders up to the top of Petrin Hill for days on end. Without machinery or anything. Oh! it is too sad. Aaoow. We carve our initials into one of the rocks with my boyfriend's Swiss Army Knife. It is a gesture of solidarity.

Prague 3 contains student accommodation. I know this because I spend a night there, even though I am no student. I stay in the dorm, in an empty room vacated by a friend of my boyfriend's for the night. We stay there together and I wish I could remember more of it but the truth is I don't. I do remember that he says, You are the first older woman I am with (he is eighteen; I am twenty-one). He also says, I suppose you have read *Unbearable Lightness of Fucking Being*. And, When I have a girlfriend my studies go well and my room is tidier. He spent last summer in New York – actually in Queens, working in a Greek restaurant. It did not improve his English. He says, I know the black slang – fuck you, motherfucker. I laugh. He is nice. He is sweet. He blinks slowly and he waits for a taxicab with me in the morning. You should take the tram, he says, which is a million kroner cheaper than a taxi, but I have never taken a tram in this city before and I am not going to start now. It is enough of a struggle to get back to where the hotel is and find Hal and Dick without this tram business. He kisses me goodbye and I cry in the taxicab because I am lost and he was nice and sweet and I am not sure where I am going to find Dick and Hal and what sort of mood they will be in when finally I do.

Places where Hal and Dick are not. They are not at the hotel. They are not at Globe. They are not at FX. I think I see them on Charles Bridge but it is not them, just two Australians who look worried when I cry. I have to find them. Whale. Globe. FX. I even go to Chapeau Rouge but it's too early and there's nobody there but the bar staff and a girl smoking a pipe. (It is a good look, and one to consider adopting later.) Where could they be? I ring the hotel and when the receptionist hears me talking she hangs up. I am lost in a city where I don't speak the language and I can't find my only two friends in the whole world. This must be the price of casual sex – my eighteen-year-old, whose name I didn't ever quite hear properly. I need somebody to hold my hands.

In Vietnam, Dick told us, there are beggars who bang their heads on the ground, harder and harder until you pay them to stop.

In Chapeau Rouge again I find them. They have not been back to the hotel. They are still on their bender. Welcome to the lost weekend, they tell me. You naughty, naughty girl, what are you doing out of your room? Dick has two Swedish girls on his arm and Hal is sulking. He is out of Marlboros and is smoking the local brand which he complains is ripping his throat to shreds. Dick has been beating him at backgammon, drinking and girls. I tell them what I've been doing and they berate me for half an hour about the dangers of unknown boys, unknown drugs, unknown addresses and unprotected sex. I didn't mean to tell them about that bit but I'm so happy to have found them I don't care.

Don't care was made to care, Hal tells me.

Yes, says Dick. Don't care was hung.

We have to see Dick to the airport. I don't like city airports, always on the edge of town past flat rust-coloured buildings and low trees. I don't like seeing so much asphalt all in one place. Big airport hotels. Hangars, and shuttle buses. Rental car places. Corrugated iron manufacturers. I know it's not fashionable to think nature is beautiful and that these man-made monstrosities are a waste of space. You're so un-modern, Hal will say. This is the future, this is real. You are such a girl.

We all cry a little, saying goodbye. Well, we make the sounds of crying and that's enough. Dick is going to Kingston, Jamaica. My heart is down, he sings, My head is spinning around.

But that's the leaving Kingston song, I say, not the leaving Prague song.

There is no leaving Prague song, he says, because I am too

bowed with grief for music.

Oh, I sigh, and feel a single tear running down my cheek.

Huh, says Hal.

Goodbye, says Dick.

Au revoir! Au revoir!

To comfort ourselves we take a walk by the river. It is grey, and glimmering (it never stops glimmering). We see a man fishing down a grating with a hat out to collect money. There is slightly too much of this sad-eye clown culture in Prague, if you ask me. Paintings on velvet, puppets on string – that sort of thing.

Take my picture, I tell Hal.

I pose next to the fishing clown and look mournful. We have six rolls of black & white film. It is très romantique. Me on the Charles Bridge, me with the Vltava in the background, me in front of the cathedral. Très Juliette Binoche. We don't take photographs of Hal. Il est trop laide. We did take some of Dick, Dick and me in pornographic contortions in our hotel room. We can sell them to the taxi drivers if we ever run out of money. This won't happen. Not as long as we stay in Eastern Europe.

What are you feeling, Hal asks me, surprisingly, back at the hotel. What are you feeling? F.e.e.l.i.n.g.

I shrug, giggling.

Search me!

Hal can sniff out an exhibition opening at twenty paces, in any city. They are the same the world over, unlike poetry readings. The tricky part is timing it so's you're not conspicuous out-of-towners, but not getting there so late that all the free drink is gone. We throw back as much as we can, look at the art a bit, and leave. This show involves a lot of perspex and fluorescent light. It's conceptual. We don't understand the concept. There is a cultural divide.

Hal is losing patience with my spouting of inside knowledge of the Czech people, gleaned from the night I spent with my sex slav. He accuses me of trying to make the best of a botched situation. Yes?, I say, not sure quite what is wrong with that. It comes out that he is still cross with me for doing it, that he thinks I took a stupid risk, that he believes 'it's different for girls', i.e. worse, and that as he's responsible for me I should respect his wishes. Then he actually says, 'act your age not your shoe size'. Excuse me? Hello? He can't tell me to grow up. I'm twenty-one. I am grown up! But I do shut up, mainly because I've repeated everything the sex slav and his friends told me and everything I've read in *Laughable Loves* (which after all is fiction, and quite old) and I've run out of inside knowledge about the Czech culture. Damn.

I miss Dick. No amount of cajoling or wheedling would persuade him to delay his ticket. Have I been let down by him? Yes. Has he used me? It's dawning on me that, most probably, he has. It's not that I thought it was love or anything, I just felt like – we had a special bond. The time when we snuck away from Hal and ate sausages in Wenceslas Square, and Dick said that Prague was the most romantic city in the world and I held my breath, then had to let it out after a minute because nothing happened . . . The times when I'm sure I caught him looking at me in a certain kind of way . . . The enthusiasm he showed for our dirty photo session . . . I could have been wrong. I must have been too gullible. I have no instinct about Dick. Perhaps I'll get back to the hotel and find a one-way ticket to Jamaica waiting for me. It's possible, after all; anything is possible!

I can see myself marrying someone like Dick – I can imagine the wedding, the honeymoon, the drink and the infidelities. The reconciliations, the anti-depressants, the children and the diets.

The trial separations, the therapy. Dick reminds me of Robert Wagner. The glamour.

Huh, says Hal, when I confess my marital fantasy over vodkas at HP (a mistake, both the venue and the confession), You've been reading too many novels. And now I am confused because the old argument used to be that I didn't read enough! Hal is hard to please. I tell him so – it seems to please him.

How long is it since I've seen the sea? I wake up, adrenaline racing through me. Hal, I say, Hal, how far away from the ocean are we? He snores and rolls over. We have a map. I dig it out of the suitcase and spread it over my bed. In the faint light I can make out where we are. Then Hungary, Romania, Black Sea. Austria, Italy, Adriatic Sea. Germany, Netherlands, North Sea. Poland, Baltic Sea – the shortest route. We're surrounded on all sides. The room is extra hot. My hands are prickling. I don't want the river. I don't want some dead old spa town or a lake. I want the ocean, the Pacific Ocean. The new world. This never-ending stone oppresses me. The cobbled streets, the ruins, the ancient tombs – it's all so much dust. You can have it. It smells like decay and chalk. Boulders being carried up mountains. Wake up, Hal, wake up.

Hey, says Hal, I know. Let's change all our money and become zloty millionaires. Ha ha ha.

I'd rather be travelling with the fishing clown than be travelling with this. I mean it.

I thought I saw Dick today, in the little café on the steps above the castle. We'd been looking at the tomb of Vladimir the Torturer, or whatever his name is. Again. Crypt after crypt, monument after monument, one fascinating piece of history after another. The guy I thought was Dick was actually the tour guide. You never know.

An old American man who has been hitting on me follows us out of Chapeau Rouge. Gross. He's forty at least. He totters along the street after us while we giggle, ignoring him. He's muttering something. We stop so we can hear what it is. He catches up with us, looks confused as if he's trying to remember where he knows us from. I lean towards him, into the mutter.

Is Roxy open. Is Roxy open. Is Roxy open.

This is what he has to say.

We walk through Unpronounceable Square for breakfast at Cornucopia.

What do you want to do today? asks Hal.

Go to the beach, I say.

Ha ha ha.

We go shopping. I buy a beret and Hal buys a fridge magnet, though we do not own a fridge. We walk up to the Globe, we read English magazines and play backgammon. We drink coffee and all the time I'm thinking the sea, the sea. The white light of home, the smell of salt and coconut oil, hot rubber and woodsmoke. Summer music from a car stereo. Roller blades and pohutukawa flowers, green hills and the green horizon of the sea.

You are as drunk as a rainbow. That's another thing the sex slav said to me, that I'd forgotten. I'm not quite sure what it means – only, I suppose (an educated guess) that you are very, very drunk.

I am sick in the toilet at Roxy. I splash my face with cold water the way men do and tell myself it's only motion sickness.

"Pickpockets," Dick was fond of telling me, "prefer to work in a tight squeeze. It arises especially in department stores." Then he'd kiss my cheek. Just remember that, honey, he'd say, they like nothing more than a tight squeeze. Ha ha ha. Diky, Dick.

Do you understand, says Hal, holding my hands in the hot

hotel room, that we can't go back yet?

My teeth are chattering.

Look at me, he says. Do. You. Understand.

He waits. I nod my head, yes.

OK, he says. OK. Tomorrow we'll take the train to Budapest. Smile!

We go to Budapest. We go.

Scenes from a Long Distance Relationship

Peter Ho Davies

Peter Ho Davies is an Anglo-Chinese writer living in the United States. His fiction and nonfiction have appeared in *Best American Short Stories* 1995 & 1996, the *Paris Review* and *Grand Tour*. His collection of short stories, *The Ugliest House in the World*, was published in 1997.

How long is long enough?

I'm watching *When Harry Met Sally* in a movie house in Singapore, surrounded in the darkness by young Chinese couples. It's a date movie and I'm with Magdalena, one of my fellow editors, but she's just a friend. (Her fiancé, Clint, is doing his national service; my girlfriend, Amanda, is in college back in England.) But Maggie and I share a passion for going to the movies – she as an escape from the flat she still shares with her parents, me as a temporary refuge from the background radiation of homesickness.

Tonight, though, the movie, with its knowing, lover's jokes, is making me miss Amanda.

There is laughter and then an odd tension in the audience. A waiting stillness. Harry and Sally are in a restaurant. They're talking about sex. It's *that* scene and everyone is holding their breath to see what will happen. Not literally what will happen in the movie, but what the government censor – immune to movie violence, but famously strict about sex – will allow to happen.

"Here it comes," someone whispers behind me. "The orgasm scene."

"The *fake* orgasm," someone else (his girlfriend?) giggles back.

And there it is and we all laugh with relief. There is even a smattering of applause. Afterwards, Maggie and I step out into the warm night air of Raffles Place and give our verdict. "Pretty funny, lah," Maggie says and I nod, although we both feel the movie's been a little over-hyped. Even the big scene wasn't *that* funny, but we were glad to see it and laughed along with everyone else. Maybe, I think, as we go our separate ways, it was funnier for couples.

But next morning, during a break from my work simplifying and condensing the classics of English literature for ESL readers, I run into Derek, our sales manager. He's seen the movie over the weekend too – and thinks it's hilarious to call it *When Hally Met Sarry*. He'd also caught some of the movie on a flight to the US. "And you know," he tells me now, "I could swear that scene was longer on the plane. You know, she faked it longer. It was *much* funnier."

I shake my head and wonder if he could be right, but even the suspicion makes me feel cheated. Cheated of the famous, international joke. Back at my desk, I can't get the idea of the censor out of my head. The censor sitting and thinking and determining that yes, it's fine for women to fake orgasm, but only for so long. Only in moderation.

This is the kind of thing that makes it easy to stay faithful in Singapore, I tell myself.

The way we left it
Amanda and I had only been going out for six weeks when I got the chance to work abroad, and although we were together for another three months, the relationship always felt provisional until the last aching days before my departure. I remember when I told her I'd got the job – excited, like an idiot, with my news – the way her face crumpled into a tiny smile. We decided to make the most of our final few weeks together, and say goodbye, but in the end we promised to keep in touch – not exactly to wait *for* each other, but at least to wait and see. Maybe the job wouldn't work out. Maybe I'd hate it out there. Maybe we'd even miss each other too much.

"We just have to swear to be honest with each other," Amanda said.

And that's the way we left it. Each promising to tell the other if we met someone else.

Perks

Of course, there are temptations. Derek at a sales meeting at the Equatorial has a note slipped across the table to him. *Room 505. Nine p.m. Two girls.* "It's just part of doing business out here," he tells me after making sure I know he's declined the offer. "A perk. Like lunch or a round of golf. It's just hospitality." It sounds to me like Derek's thinking about it, but then he's not got anyone waiting at home.

A few weeks later, he's at a conference in Bangkok, at a banquet with a cabaret of dancing girls. Not the chesty Aussies who occasionally tour Singapore but slim Asian girls. One of them sits on his knee and he puts his arm around her waist. Later he finds out she's a boy. "It's how they earn money for the sex change op, apparently," he says, shaking his head. "Thank goodness I didn't kiss him like everyone wanted." He means his sales team. Derek is the office joke for a few days, but he's good-natured about it. "You have to be able to take a bit of stick," he tells me. We're the only Brits in the office, so we get our share of leg-pulling.

"Of course," he says, suddenly suspicious, "they only *told* me it was a boy. Who knows?" He shrugs. "Buggered if I could tell."

Self-censorship

In the last few months Amanda and I have discovered a mutual clumsy talent for sexual fantasy.

It started when I was working in Malaysia, before coming to

Singapore. International phone calls were hopeless from KL. There was a painful delay on the line and a throbbing echo that made you feel like you were talking to yourself. So we started writing letters – two or three pale blue aerogrammes a week – and began our second relationship.

There just wasn't enough *news* for two or three letters a week, not even for me, starting a new job in a new country, and certainly not for Amanda, still home in England. At first we wrote about how we felt, discovering in the process how much easier it is to write 'love' in letters from the other side of the world. But then, just when we were starting to congratulate ourselves on this new honesty, we found there are only so many ways to say how much you miss someone. We began to write about our fantasies instead. Pretty soon we were bound by something new: a shared, sickly sweet embarrassment.

We write about all the things we'd like to do to each other. All the things we've been too reluctant to try together. She sends me letters she's pressed to her lip-sticked lips, doused in perfume she rarely wears. The scented letters crackle in my hands, brittle from being damp and then dried, but the fragrance, when I slit them open, is heady.

Together we would censor such thoughts and language. Alone – apart – we indulge ourselves. It's no wonder neither of us meets anyone else.

Going JB

My turn for some office leg-pulling comes when my visa runs out. It's a tourist visa and I've been working on it for two months while my official work authorisation comes through, but now it's almost up and the new permit is still a few weeks from being processed. I mention the problem around the office and a solution soon presents itself. Malaysia is only six miles away across the causeway. If I go there and come back I'll get a new tourist stamp, good for another month, long enough for the permit to be approved. It just so happens that two of Derek's salesmen, Jimmy and George, make the occasional trip across the border to Johore Bahru, the town on the Malaysian side, and they volunteer to take me this Friday. "Sure," George says with a huge wink. "You come JB with us. Good time, man." And he laughs, and without knowing what I'm laughing at I laugh too.

And this is the way the week goes. Maggie and her fellow editors giggle and ask me if I'm really *going JB* with Jimmy and George. Even Derek gets in on the act. "Think of England," he tells me in mock encouragement. In the bathroom, Mr Woo, the accountant, stands beside me at the urinal and says, "I hear you go JB with Jimmy and George next time." He sounds mournful and I know he wishes the fellows would invite him.

I ask Maggie if there's anything to all this teasing and she perches on the edge of my desk and says she doesn't think so. George is married and Jimmy engaged. Maggie peers at the framed photo of Amanda that sits like a shield on my desk. "*Ho leng,*" she says. "So pretty, already." And she beams. "Like Princess Di!"

Maggie, despite her bright blouses and taut mini skirts, is born-again, and something about this unlikely combination of faith and fashion makes me believe her. But just before we leave that night, Mr Tan, the manager, takes me aside.

"You're going JB with Jimmy and George?"

I nod.

"Just be careful," he says darkly.

Talking dirty

Since I arrived in Singapore Amanda and I have been talking on the phone more regularly. Once a week, on my way to work, I buy a S$20 phonecard and call her from the bright, spotless ticket hall of the Clementi MRT stop. At 7 a.m. in Singapore it's midnight in England. The connection is crisp – almost uncannily so – but these calls are still difficult. We never know what to say. I'm dazed and apprehensive about another day in the office, surrounded by a tide of commuters, watching the credit on my phonecard run down. Amanda is tired too, but at the end of her day. We're hopelessly out of sync.

After our letters, our calls feel so bloodless. What movies we've seen, gossip about friends, my visa situation, her courses. She asks me about work and I tell her I'm finishing *A Tale of Two Cities*, about to start on *Lord Jim*. We tell ourselves it's important to preserve this casual, everyday part of the relationship, but then what's this slight disappointment in our voices?

The first time I called, we tried to talk dirty to each other.

"Hi, lover," I whispered, but I felt like a fool.

"Hello, darling," she breathed back, and we both cringed inwardly.

"What are you wearing?" I managed, blushing furiously but feeling that I should ask.

"My dressing gown," she said, mercifully, and we dropped the subject. Now we're more coy.

"I got your last letter," I say, and she giggles.

"Mine's on the way," I tell her. "I think you'll like it."

It's as if we can't wait to get off the phone and back to our letters.

The unspoken reason why these calls are awkward is that I haven't yet decided if I'm staying in Singapore or coming home, making a career in the Pacific Rim or just getting 'experience'. We aren't sure if we're people who have been lovers, or people who are going to be lovers again, if our letters are about the past or the future. Amanda has never asked me to leave, although it's all I'm waiting for. I need to know she wants me back, but she needs to know I want to come back. It's an impasse, but we've been apart for almost six months now and I'm starting to feel I have an obligation to decide one way or the other. I picture myself balanced on the Pacific Rim.

The blur of numbers on the phone approaches zero.

"I'm going to get cut off soon," I warn her. This is our cue.

"I love you," we tell each other.

"I miss you," we reply.

The Crystal Palace

In JB Jimmy and George take me to dinner first – chilli crab, fish-head curry, sea slug, all the challenging delicacies. "Can take?" Jimmy asks me with a grin. "Good or not?" and I tell him, "Delicious." Then, with much laughter, they announce it's time for a 'shampoo'. I sit in the back of the car trying to work out the euphemism as we drive through the night, but in the end they mean it literally.

We go to a gleaming chrome and marble salon and Jimmy and George have their hair washed while I have a wash and a cut. The shampoo is wonderful, a deep, sudsy scalp massage by a gorgeous hairdresser, and when I'm done I feel clean and relaxed. Pampered. My head, shorn and scrubbed, tingles.

And then we get back in the car and Jimmy says, "Crystal Palace?" and George says, "Yes-one-ah."

The Crystal Palace is the darkest place I've ever seen. George knocks at a door in a shadowy sidestreet and speaks into the small hatch that slides back. When the door opens we shuffle into a profound darkness. A cigarette lighter strikes in front of me and we follow the tiny flame to a high-sided booth and slide in. George, then me, then Jimmy. The lighter flicks on and off twice and a bottle of 'Napoleon' brandy and three glasses appear at the table. George slides a fifty dollar note across the table and it vanishes into the darkness. The brandy tastes like weak medicine. "Sour water," Jimmy laughs.

The place reminds me of a movie house. There's the same sense of a crowd in the darkness. The warmth and scent and sound of many bodies, breathing and rustling. And gradually as my eyes grow accustomed I see that the walls are lined with girls. A few are naked, most in short, shiny kimonos. A group drift towards our booth.

"Hello ladies," George sings, waving them over. He slaps the vinyl seat beside him. "Come and sit."

"Which?" a girl asks, stepping forward. Her kimono hangs open from breasts to thighs.

"Too old, man," Jimmy breaks in. "Go home, auntie."

George points to a second girl and she comes forward and he takes her on to his knee. Another is passed over Jimmy to sit in my lap and Jimmy pulls a third into his arms. Except they're not girls. Not mine anyway, and not George's. They're older, older than me, certainly. George's has shed her kimono already and mine is wriggling her shoulders to do the same until I put my arm around her. I stroke her back, but she turns round and takes my hand and clasps it to her faintly clammy breast, where I leave it, afraid to move, afraid to take it away, afraid to insult her.

Jimmy has no such qualms. He's laughing at his girl. He's found she's wearing a bra and is snapping the elastic. "Must be new," he tells us. "A bra!" he roars. I look at the girl on his knee and she is absolutely impassive, glum. Jimmy asks how old she is. She won't answer him when he asks her in English, but when he asks her in Cantonese she replies dully. "She say eighteen," Jimmy tells me, but he's shaking his head. "Thirteen, fourteen maybe," he guesses.

I tell him to ask her her name but he says, "For what?"

"Then ask her why she does it." He just looks at me like I'm a moron.

"Why?" he laughs. "Why else, man? For the fucking money."

He slips one of her breasts out of her bra, cups it, bounces it in his hand. "Small or what? Not like English girl."

George is talking about going upstairs, but first he needs to find a girl for me. The one I had before has gone, sliding away, tired of me. Another appears between my legs, crawling up from under the table to fill my lap. She is naked and damp with sweat. She puts her head on my shoulder and, after a moment, takes my hand in hers and slips it between her thighs. "You like?" George is saying. "Sure! Bring her upstairs."

And then his pager goes off and in the darkness I see the green light of its display as he toggles the button.

"Shit," he says at length.

"What, lah?" Jimmy wants to know.

"My wife," George says, instantly defeated.

And that's that. George has told his wife he's working late. She'll expect him to call back, and has probably already called the office. He can tell her he was out, but he needs to call her soon.

"So call, lah," Jimmy says.

"How can?" George asks him.

He can't call from Malaysia because she'll know it's an international call.

And if she knows he's in JB she'll know why.

And it's forty minutes for us to get back across the causeway.

So that's that and I'm spared, although I'm not sure what. Perhaps it was all just an elaborate joke the boys were playing on me. Perhaps upstairs would have been just a show. Something crudely comic with bananas and ping-pong balls and lit cigarettes. A magic act with a vagina for a top hat. But perhaps it would have been me alone with the girl on my lap, having to decide what I wanted. Could I have told her no? Maybe, so long as I'd paid. But who can be sure? Perhaps I'd have felt obliged in some way. Embarrassed for her. Perhaps I'd have been tempted to fake my lust.

Counting down

This week on the phone to Amanda I tell her I've decided – I'm leaving at the end of the month as soon as I can finish the current project. "*Romeo and Juliet*," I tell her and she laughs and begins to cry softly as I watch my credit count down. To distract her I talk about what we'll do in the summer. We start to make plans, a long holiday together, a cottage in France perhaps, just the two of us.

The numbers in the liquid-crystal display race towards zero.

"I'm going to get cut off soon," I warn, but suddenly she asks, "Oh, how did that visa thing go?" I pause as my last dollar ticks away. For a second I think I could tell her, make it a joke between us. But there's no time. "Fine," I say, and then quickly, "I love you."

"I miss you," she says.

And then because there are a few more cents on the phonecard I take a breath to say something else and – click, she's gone.

My card pops out and suddenly I'm back in the station, on

my way to work, hanging up the phone. I pluck out the card and stare at it, expecting it to somehow look different now that it's used up, but it's the same.

P.S.

We've written so many letters about what we'll do when we see each other again, the moment is an anticlimax. We haven't changed so much after all, and we don't talk about, let alone act on, our fantasies. The closest we come is Amanda posing in the silk cheongsam I bring back, her thigh impossibly pale in the long, high slit. I take a photograph and she never wears it again.

Travelling three thousand miles for someone, we find, is not a happy ending, just a start. Friends and parents look at us with broad, approving smiles when they see us together again, and then slowly as the weeks pass with more impatience. We feel it ourselves. What's next? we wonder. Where do we go from here?

The short answer is Provence, where our plans for a holiday cottage begin to assume new proportions: an experiment in living together; a trial period. But in France, we finally unravel. We make up separate beds in the tiny cottage. Scowl in photographs. Go days without speaking.

Amanda, I discover, is afraid of spiders and mice. My only abiding use to her seems to be disposing of them. One night, before bed, I put her hairbrush at the bottom of the bed we don't share any more and lie in wait for her screams through the thin plasterboard, grinning in anticipation. But all I hear is the soft pad of her bare feet on the cool tiles, approaching my door. "Good one," she tells me, hurling the brush at my head. "Ha-bloody-ha."

Ashamed, I tell myself it would have been funnier if we were still a couple, but we're not even sharing jokes now. Instead, separately – together – we lie awake in the warm, still night, listening to each other's breathing, tangling our sheets, longing for the distance of our long-distance relationship.

from
The Weather Prophet

Lucretia Stewart

Lucretia Stewart was born in Singapore in 1952. She is the author of *Tiger Balm* and *The Weather Prophet: A Caribbean Journey*.

I was going to Marie-Galante – a small, virtually round island devoted to the cultivation of sugar cane, some twenty-five miles from the mainland – at the suggestion of Abdul, the waiter from Djibouti. He said that it was very unspoiled, 'très tranquille, vraiment Creole'. There was, however, nothing tranquil about the crossing. The sea was very rough, there were huge waves, and the boat, a sort of catamaran, like that I had taken from Dominica to Martinique, had (despite its state-of-the-art appearance) sprung a leak just over my seat. I was still too bruised from my last sea outing to risk another fall, so I sat rigid in my wet seat, feeling violently sick and longing for the crossing to end.

Saint-Louis, Marie-Galante's second port, is a one-horse town. Its only hotel, Le Salut, lies within easy walking distance of the quay, its view of the sea obscured by the *hôtel de ville*. There was room there, plenty of it. The only other guest was an elderly French scientist, who was studying the flora and fauna of Marie-Galante. He was on his eighteenth visit and was still finding new species. The manager, Johnny, a young man with wide, startled eyes like a fawn, showed me to a corner room on the top floor. It was simple, clean and pretty and I liked it very much. A broad balcony ran round the hotel and, from it, I could observe the comings and goings of Saint-Louis.

The quay led directly into one of the two main roads which ran through the town, past two or three grocery stores, a couple of small restaurants, the post office, the school and a large unfinished sports stadium, then on up into the hills which lay between Saint-Louis and Capesterre on the Atlantic coast. The other road, parallel to the sea, ran past Le Salut, the police station and the *hôtel de ville*, then on past a few rum shops and restaurants – one, Chez Raoul, looked a cut above the rest.

In the gaps between the buildings, you could see the sea – limpid, molten. Both roads led, more or less directly, to the island's capital, Grand-Bourg, merging just before the sugarcane factory. From the sea front, the town rose in a gentle slope to a grid of residential streets, to which the inhabitants of Saint-Louis presumably retreated at night. To the uninitiated, every street looked the same: Rue Martin Luther King might as well have been Rue John Kennedy. From my terrace, I could see across the galvanise rooftops to the fields of sugar cane beyond. I walked up the road to one of the restaurants.

Over lunch I got into conversation with a Rasta who wanted to show me the sights; he said that I simply had to get up at dawn to see the sunrise at Capesterre. A Swiss, sitting at the next table, offered to come and give me a massage – for my bruises. He had been a long-distance lorry driver and said that he had made a lot of money on the stock exchange. One day, in Basle, the Swiss said, he was on his motorbike with his daughter riding pillion. As he was going through a green light at a crossroads, an Englishman in a car jumped a red light and hit him full on. He lay in the road for two hours and then spent the next forty-eight in a coma. This had taken place eighteen months ago and he had never been right since; his back and his legs pained him constantly, he had lost his memory, he had epileptic fits. The insurance company refused to pay up, because its doctor said that he had been ill (perhaps epileptic) before the accident. He had had to sell his lorry, his car and his motorbike – he could no longer drive; his marriage had broken up. In the winter, when the weather was cold, his legs refused to work so he had to go to the sun. He had come to Marie-Galante to fish. He kept his watch set at Swiss time because he said that time meant nothing in the Antilles. He said that the people in Marie-Galante didn't know how lucky they were – they got all this money from France, and sometimes they were so insolent.

As the evening drew in and the light turned soft and rosy, the hills around seemed to glow, then blur – and then seemed to almost pulsate. Across from the parking lot, which flanked the hotel, loud reggae music burst suddenly from a little house. With a fast gear change, a battered red car pulled into the lot and a black man got out and crossed the road to Chez Raoul. He unlocked its door, disappeared inside and, minutes later, it lit up and music exploded from it; later that evening I took Johnny there for dinner.

The owner of Chez Raoul was Johnny's cousin. He had been born in Marie-Galante, in what was now his restaurant, but his mother had taken him to Toulon at the age of seven months. As a result of that, Raoul spoke French with a strong – and to me almost incomprehensible – Provençal accent. People whose first language was Creole (divine gurgling) had a sort of nasal timbre but Raoul was just gruff; he spoke almost no Creole. He was thirty-seven and had been back in Marie-Galante for ten years. When he had returned the family house was in ruins; he had had to rebuild the whole thing. He seemed to me to be different from other Caribbean men. Perhaps it was something to do with having grown up in France which gave him an edge over other local people, but I think he had something less easily definable. I suppose he was 'cool' – both aloof and hip. He made no effort to please and he rationed his somewhat ferocious charm – which, when he chose to exercise it, could be considerable. He was medium height, dark-skinned, but not black, black. He had small ears without lobes, a gap between his front teeth and his skull seemed to flow into his neck, which flowed into his body. He was slender, but intensely muscular, and moved like a big cat, seemingly utterly relaxed.

His restaurant was beautiful, it had a white tiled floor and a ceiling of split bamboo; it was surrounded by wooden shutters which could be propped open on bamboo poles so that the dining room gave immediately onto the beach; a hammock swung between two palm trees; beyond it was the sea. Saint-Louis faced west, and at sunset the water was bathed in gold. When it was dark the single lamp-post at the end of the quay cast a slender column of pale light across to the shore. Johnny and I were the only customers. There was a small, steel-grey, tabby cat prowling around. Raoul shooed it away roughly. When I protested, he said, "Ne t'inquiète pas. Je ne frappe pas les femmes." We ate some swordfish in a sauce of cream and sage and, when we had finished, we all climbed into Raoul's battered red car and drove through the starry night down to Grand-Bourg.

El Moana, a pizzeria-cum-bar, run by a *métropolitain* with a weak, amiable face, was full. A Frenchman covered with tattoos leant against the bar and a black woman called Nicole with a rat's-tail of a plait, wearing sexy shorts, was speaking French with an accent which I couldn't place. I asked her where she came from. And she said Paris, New York, London – and now she was in Marie-Galante.

It was late when we got back to Saint-Louis. As I started up the stairs to my room, Johnny grabbed my arm, saying surely I didn't plan to leave him all on his own. I freed myself – said I most certainly did – and locked my door behind me.

The next day when I went to the beach Johnny followed me in his jeep, but after I let him know how much this irritated me he stopped – or seemed to stop – wanting to know my every movement. But he was a strange man, and for long periods of time the hotel was locked up with no one around even to answer the telephone. One afternoon he told me that he didn't like most people, then said: "Can I ask you something?"

"Yes, of course."

"You seem very nice and you appear to get on with everybody. Are you really like that or is it just because of your work?"

I didn't know what to tell him. I didn't know the answer myself.

By daylight, Grand-Bourg was just another dusty Caribbean town. Many of its older buildings had been destroyed by a fire in 1901 and, on the whole, the architecture was nondescript. Fortunately, the church, Notre Dame de Marie-Galante, has survived. Built in 1827, it has a vaulted wooden ceiling painted a bright sky-blue – almost the colour of the punch in Pointe-à-Pitre – and an elaborate marble altar with a bas-relief of the Last Supper. The stained-glass windows are modern and, I thought, ugly. A long street full of shabby shops, selling shoes and postcards and bolts of cloth, ran from the steps of the church past the little market down to the port. A building with wooden shutters and a cool interior was the domain of the *Ecrivain Public*, a French woman, who was open for business from eight to twelve, Monday to Friday, and on Saturday *sur rendez-vous*. The *Ecrivain Public* wrote letters for people, mainly business letters, but she also helped with contracts and other legal matters. The *hôtel de ville*, a white Thirties' building, was in a pretty tree-lined square with benches for old men to doze on; there were

225

three or four palatial *pharmacies*, all plate-glass and chrome, full of homoeopathic remedies for disorders of the blood and liver; there was also an astonishing number of elegant little restaurants. In the market I heard a woman say, "J'ai perdu tout mon espoir."

*

In Saint-Louis I met a couple of French students, Rashid and Fred. They had taken a year off from their studies to work for a fisherman from Les Saintes and were trying to save enough money to get to Venezuela. But their wages depended on the daily catch and I doubted that they would manage it. Rashid, a Kabyle originally from Algeria, was dark, deeply tanned and handsome in a flashy James Dean way. He was twenty-two, a business student. Fred, aged twenty, had ginger hair bleached almost white and skin that couldn't take the sun. Rashid was the leader, the one with more confidence. They were very nice, very young and had beautiful manners. I asked them if I could go fishing with them one morning and they said that they would have to ask the *patron*. That evening they came to the hotel and said that their *patron* wanted to meet me.

The fisherman, Gerard, was white, a Saintois, a descendant of the Les Saintes Breton fishermen who rarely marry outside their race and colour. (The rocky, arid terrain of Les Saintes had prohibited the cultivation of sugar cane and there had therefore been no need for slaves.) Gerard said that his grandmother had been black, but looking at his blue eyes and straw-coloured hair, you could not tell. He was in his late forties, though years of exposure to the sun, wind and sea had made him look older. He had been fishing off Marie-Galante for twenty-five years. But the water round Les Saintes was now, he said, all fished out; from

Tuesday to Saturday he fished off Marie-Galante, then returned to his wife and family in Les Saintes for long weekends; he had built a house with twenty-five rooms there, which he ran as a hotel. His brother operated a boat shuttle service between Les Saintes and Trois Rivières in Basse-Terre. He said he had five children – all of them, according to him, splendid-looking, particularly the girls – "Je fais très belles nanas," he boasted; but he had never once been around for one of his wife's *accouchements*. Grizzled, bearded, muscular, with legs like tree trunks, he sat at the table in his little wooden shack, a bottle of the lethal 65% proof Père Labat white rum of the island in front of him. We had a couple of drinks and he said that I could go with them the following morning. He also said that I must have been very beautiful when I was young and that he wished he had known me then.

When the alarm went off at a quarter to five, the sky outside was as black as could be. I dressed, and, just before five, walked along the sleeping road to Gerard's house. There wasn't a soul about. The faint roar of a motorcycle in the distance, the sounds of dogs barking and cocks crowing, the pink plastic leg of a doll abandoned in the dirt were the only evidence of life.

Gerard was up and ready and suggested that we go and get a cup of coffee in town. There was no sign of the boys, so we walked back down the road; behind the hills, towards Capesterre, a faint luminous glow was already beginning to colour the sky.

In the little café opposite the market there were already a couple of customers downing a quick *décollage* before setting out to sea. As I drank my coffee, black, strong and sweet, Raoul's brother, Baptiste, came in for a quick early-morning jolt of rum. He had the sore red eyes of a heavy drinker – what is known as a 'rumbo' in the English islands.

Back at the shack, the boys, yawning, stumbling and rubbing their eyes, were as ready to go as they would ever be. We waded through the tide, then set out in two boats: Gerard, the two students and two young, local, black men in one; a tall slim black, named Lytho, and me in the other. Gerard, in a battered sombrero and oil-stained polo shirt, his waist cinched with a broad leather belt, looked like a pirate. Lytho, in a wetsuit with a balaclava hood, looked like a Martian.

Fishing requires patience. That soon became clear. We motored out into deep water, off Grand-Bourg, and cast the net. Two boats were necessary because they trawled the net between them. The students jumped into the water and swam alongside the little buoys which held the net afloat. Gerard steered one boat and Lytho the other. One of the men in Gerard's boat put on a mask and swam ahead, driving the fish back into the long net. The two boats began far apart, then drew closer, closing the circle of the net and pulling it and its contents towards one of the boats. We repeated this five times, and in the east, beyond Capesterre, the sun began to rise. There were long periods of apparent inactivity, but it was pleasant enough to be out on the sea and to watch the day unfold and the dark outline of the island take on character and definition as the sun came up. By the time we were through, it was broad daylight. As we sat in the boat and waited, Lytho talked to me.

He talked about Buddhism, about the Dalai Lama and about mammals. He said that he liked to make 'spiritual' love, that Saintois men treat their women like queens, that he adored his girlfriend – a half-French, half-Brazilian white woman – but that, at thirty-nine, she was too old to have children and she had been around; later that day I saw her (she was either lying about her age or had been to hell and back). I asked him whether you could see any whales near Trois Rivières. "Yes," he said; there were some calves. I asked how long the whale's gestation period was. He said nine months – just like a woman. I was surprised that it was so short (in fact, it takes between eleven and sixteen months, depending on the species) and asked why, therefore, it could take nearly two years for an elephant to come to term. He said that that was because elephants aren't real mammals – unlike whales. He also volunteered that Raoul was 'un peu lourd' – that he could be 'très gentil', but also, on bad days, 'très méchant'.

From the point of view of fishing, the expedition was a disappointment. Cast after cast yielded an almost empty net. At one point the man in the water saw a huge shoal, but then it swam out of reach. It looked as if Rashid and Fred's trip to Venezuela would have to be postponed. But, with our final throw, we pulled in a small load of silvery *orfie* (ocean gar, or needlefish); they had long pointed beaks and little sharp teeth serrated like a bread knife. Everyone looked relieved.

As we got back to Saint-Louis a school bus drew up and disgorged a crowd of small children by the Ecole de Voile. They rushed on to the beach, shrieking like baby birds, and began to don life-jackets, assemble tiny boats and put up sails. Then they jumped into the boats and sailed off into the calm blue, the sound of their shrill voices drifting back across the water. Gerard sped off in the direction of Basse-Terre to sell the *orfie*.

*

One day I took the bus across to Capesterre.

Capesterre, on the Atlantic coast, was bathed in brilliant white light. From a bend in the road on the hillside above it, you could see the town laid out before you, like a series of coloured boxes;

beyond it stretched sea, crystalline, turquoise, magnificently transparent, up to the reef, where it suddenly splintered in a spray of white – beyond all was stormy, dark and deep blue. I liked the beach at Saint-Louis, strewn with conch shells, their livid interiors reminiscent of female genitalia – but Capesterre's Anse de la Feuillère was a beach from dreamland.

After lunch – cold red wine and *court-bouillon de dorade* – in a restaurant presided over by a fat man with no teeth – it turned out there were no buses and I stood by the side of the road in the full heat of the afternoon sun for twenty minutes – wondering how I was going to get back to Saint-Louis. Then the postman, in his Post Office yellow Renault 4, pulled up and offered me a lift.

The postman's name was Georges. We made a detour to feed his cow and her calf, and then he took me to see his house and his wife. The house was huge; he had built it on his return from Paris and they let rooms. He showed me photographs of their four children, who were aged between twenty and thirty, and he gave me several glasses of home-made *punch de coco*. His wife's name was Thérèse. She was very black and, initially, seemed rather out of it, but perked up after a couple of drinks; we had a lively conversation about AIDS. While Georges was out of the room, she told me that, on the whole, men didn't like condoms and wouldn't use them. (According to a report, which I later saw reprinted in an Antiguan paper, Caribbean men were all for the female condom: 'It should be less panic and easier on the man's nerves'.)

Georges drove me back to Saint-Louis, making restrained advances all the way. I told him that I never slept with married men whose wives I knew. He looked dejected and said he could see that he had made a big mistake in introducing me to Thérèse.

He said she wouldn't mind at all and started a long story designed to prove how tolerant and understanding she was. He said that when he had lived in Paris he had become involved with a young white girl. He had thought that she was over twenty-one – which was the age of consent – but actually she was only seventeen. She was mad for him, he said: she wanted to have a child by him. Her parents found out and it got ugly. Thérèse found out too, and had stuck by him, so she was unlikely to mind if he were to sleep with me.

As we drove into Saint-Louis we saw Raoul, who was getting into his car. Georges said:

"Oh, him, he comes from Marseilles. He's involved with drugs."

That night, after dinner, Raoul came over to the hotel. I was talking on the telephone, to a girlfriend in Washington.

When I had finished, Raoul said that he had something he wanted to show me. "And what might that be?" I said. "Ne faîtes-pas la gamine avec moi," he said, without smiling.

I couldn't decide what to do. Then I made up my mind very quickly and said, "OK, let's go."

Johnny's reproachful gaze followed me out to the car. In the car, I thought, "This is not a nice man. This is a man who doesn't like cats."

We got to his house. He made me a drink, put on some music and rolled a joint. Then he took off my clothes. I felt remote, detached, but perhaps that was the grass. He was a beautiful man, the most beautiful, I think, that I had ever seen, with a body like a coiled spring, but cool, very cool.

Afterwards I couldn't sleep and, around three, I got up and dressed in the pitch-black room. Soon after, Raoul woke and, with perfect good humour, insisted on driving me back to the hotel. I half-expected to find Johnny waiting up for me but all was dark.

The next morning I took the bus to Grand-Bourg. The Swiss came with me. He asked what I had done the night before. I said that I had gone out with Raoul. He said that he had thought of warning me against Raoul but that he had figured I was old enough to take care of myself. It gave me an odd kind of pleasure, to know I had done something of which he would have disapproved.

*

One evening Raoul drove me up into the hills. He said, "I'm going to show you the most beautiful place in the world."

Away from the coast, in the secret heart of Marie-Galante, life moved at a snail's pace; I felt as if I had taken a giant step back in time. The sugar cane was still brought to the factory in carts pulled by oxen, and scattered all over a radiant landscape were idyllic rural scenes which an English painter like Constable would have relished. There were wooden carts, their shafts resting on the ground; stray wheels were propped up against trees; cattle were grazing; the tall walls of sugar cane; a cloud drifted like smoke across the mountain; the light was both dark and golden. Land and sky at this time of day bore no relation to each other: one was dark, nether, hidden, the other was luminous and open like a child's face. The sliver of crescent moon rising in the dusk-pink sky belonged to a time of day that was neither day nor night, too pale to survive the dark, detached and pure above the voluptuous blaze of the sunset.

Raoul's friend, Christoph, was half-German and half-Guadeloupean. He looked like an Arab, with shaggy blond hair.

He lived in a wooden house that he had built himself at Etang Noire – the black lake – right in the centre of the island; it had a scented garden full of banana, hibiscus, bougainvillea and other trees and shrubs that I didn't recognise. To the west, catching the rays of the setting sun, stood a traveller's tree, its palms splayed against the light.

Here was where Raoul came to rest, to renew himself after too many late nights, too many joints, too much rum and too many women. He was guided by something he called 'le feeling' which, as far as I could understand, was part-intuition, part-instinct, and he did exactly as he pleased, making no concessions to convention, or to the wishes of others – unless those wishes coincided with his own desires. He had beautiful manners and was sometimes very flirtatious with me – and other women – but he never made small talk, nor made any attempt to put anyone at ease. He did what he wanted and he expected others to do the same. The man in El Moana had described him as 'une force de nature'.

However, even though he followed the dictates of his moods, it didn't follow that this made him happy. As I got to know him better, I realised he had a terrible temper, which, especially when he had had a lot to drink, seemed ungovernable; there was a dark side to his nature that could completely overshadow his charming side. Also he had the constitution of an ox and could emerge, fresh and reinvigorated, after a debauch that would have laid anyone else out for a week. I would tease him, saying that he was like a vampire – the way he came alive after dark. I once asked him why his relationship with the mother of his son had broken up (in French, the word for wife, *femme*, is the same as the word for woman, so you never knew, in the Antilles, whether a man was actually married). He replied that she was very jealous, adding "Moi, je suis plutôt aventurier." But Seraphine, a Dominican, who worked for him in the restaurant, said that he used to hit his wife and that was why she had gone back to France, taking the child with her.

He fascinated me. It wasn't just his beauty. He exuded power and force and his apparent total disregard for almost everything was compelling. I wasn't the only one who was mesmerised by him. Everyone in Marie-Galante was. You could tell by the way they talked about him.

Christoph was a vegetarian, almost a teetotaller; he seemed to be a sort of guru, charming and infinitely patient. He made a fairly decent living as a transpersonal astrologer (his card read 'astrologie karmique, astrologie transpersonnelle') but he was also building wooden houses, which he planned to let or sell to vegetarian tourists. I asked him why I always fell in love with Gemini men and why the result was always disastrous; he asked me for the date, time and place of my birth and looked me up on his little Toshiba laptop computer.

"Your sexuality is very important," he said. "It is the key to you. Gemini men make love with their intellect which dazzles you but you need something earthier."

There was nothing in my chart about marriage or children and he said that I would never have any money. I would get by, he said, but I would never be rich. Before we left, Christoph gave me a handful of leaves. When I crushed them in my hand, their perfume rose, sweet and fresh, into the air; it stayed in my bag for days afterwards.

As we drove away, I told Raoul what Christoph had said about Gemini men and he asked whether he had said anything about my relationship with men born under the sign of Libra – which he was. It was, I think, the nearest he came to making a remark which could be interpreted as romantic, unless you count catching me in his arms in a big hug and saying "Bella," or the time when he reproved me for saying "coucher avec" (go to bed with). "On ne dit pas 'coucher avec'. On dit 'faire l'amour'."

*

The Antilles is full of superstition of a rather perfunctory and romantic kind. A series of postcards revealed an entire Creole astrology which worked on the same date basis as the one we used but with different symbols. Thus, Sagittarius, which I am, appeared as *ouassou* (a sort of fresh-water crayfish) and Libra as pelican or *grangouzye*.

Every time I walked to the post office in Saint-Louis, in one of those little wooden houses which were being regularly checked for *Aedes aegypti* – mosquitoes which carried yellow fever and dengue fever – dozens of houses carried a little paper notice with the words: *Campagnes de lutte contre l'Aedes aegypti*. I passed a sign which advertised a soothsayer with an African name, whose card I had found at Raoul's, and who was supposed to give you advice about love and money. (In the English islands, that sort of adviser tended to have a more religious bias – Sister Hope would appear on television, offering 'direction' and a telephone number to call.)

*

After we left Christoph, we drove down through the dark, over rough roads, bordered with sugar cane, to Grand-Bourg where Raoul had been invited to dinner by a friend, a Swiss called André who owned a little restaurant near the port.

Here the atmosphere was quite different. André was a man in his forties with a big stomach who had lived in Marie-Galante for five years. He cooked like a dream (we ate a *bisque* of *ravé de mer*, then some snail-like things, followed by a *fricassée d'oursins* and finally little pots of chocolate). He made the usual jokes about English cooking – how the only decent meal you could get in England was breakfast, and so on. His philosophy of life was: "Baiser et bouffer – c'est tout qui'il y a faire dans la vie. C'est la même chose mais quand tu veillisses, tu baises moins et tu bouffes plus."

He told Raoul that I was 'much better than the last one'. Then he went to the kitchen to fetch yet another delicacy, calling back to me:

"Lucrèce, est-ce que tu aimes les noix?"

I heard '*noirs*' and, looking embarrassedly at Raoul, said: "Bien-sûr, je les aime."

André reappeared with a dish of walnuts.

Marie-Galante seemed to be full of people like André, sophisticated, *bon vivant métros* who wanted to live well and avoid the rat race. But there was nothing simple about Marie-Galante. It might seem simple, basic even, but André made his *ti punch* with honey or *coulis de framboise*; he had his ingredients flown in from Paris or Geneva and had only superficially adapted to his surroundings. In fact, he had moulded his surroundings to suit him. He told me he hated black people – though I think he was just trying to provoke me; but at least he was honest. I lost count of the number of whites in Marie-Galante who began sentences with the words: "Je ne suis pas raciste, mais . . ."

Raoul, most of whose friends were white, also had a low opinion of the local people; they drove him mad with their slowness and inefficiency. "Les gens sont cons," he would shout, crashing the gears. (He was a very bad driver, extremely short-sighted and often dangerously stoned or drunk. When he was stoned, he would simply drive very slowly, but all over the road. Fortunately there was hardly ever much traffic, but, if I drove, we would squabble – about how fast I was going or about the route.)

The life I was leading was Antillais and rarefied rather than Caribbean; it was quite stifling and I began to long for the vigour of the English-speaking islands. Each island was in a world of its own – or perhaps it was that each island was a world of its own – and on the French ones this was particularly so. I had bought a scrimshaw-carved penknife in Bequia, which Theo had admired, but he had never heard of Bequia. It had been hard to credit.

If it was sometimes tiring to make love in a foreign language, it was even harder to quarrel in one and the relationship between Raoul and myself was becoming increasingly uneasy. He had a strong narcissistic streak and was used to being worshipped. Ostensibly, he could be quite passive sexually (passive-aggressive as Americans say), or maybe he was just lazy, and I suppose my pride or sense of myself rebelled against the degree of abnegation that he seemed to demand. Beneath his sleepy exterior there was a barely controlled ferocity and it was very easy to cross him. Like a big cat, he could suddenly reach out and give me a lethal swipe with a huge paw. His caresses came to seem like blows. Perhaps it was my imagination, but I was never quite sure how much Raoul liked women – and, as always with black men, I suspected that, mingled with his desire for my whiteness, there was an almost equal loathing of it.

The night before I left Marie-Galante, a journalist from Gua-deloupe, an old friend of Raoul's, came to dine in the restaurant.

He had been born in Marie-Galante, educated in France, and now ran a weekly magazine in Pointe-à-Pitre. He had come home for a funeral. I quite liked him; he talked about politics, the economy and the independence movement – he thought that Guadeloupe should be independent. Raoul had no help that night, and was busy in the kitchen, and so, when Michel invited me to join him, I accepted. While we were waiting to eat, he suggested we might go for a walk.

The sky was a deep midnight blue, simultaneously both dark and light. The moon was hidden behind a cloud. We walked along the beach, then back past the war memorial in the square behind the *hôtel de ville*. Suddenly Michel stopped talking about politics and said:

"Sois gentille avec moi. Pourquoi tu n'es pas gentille avec moi?"

I wasn't aware that I was being anything other than *gentille*, but it was immediately obvious that he meant something else. We returned to the restaurant, and throughout dinner he continued to stare pointedly and aggrievedly at me as if I had betrayed him in some way. Suddenly, he jumped up and whispered something to Raoul, looking over his shoulder at me. When he came back and sat down again, nothing was right – neither the food nor the wine and, when he discovered that there was no Grand Marnier, he paid the bill and left in a hurry. Raoul commented on the speed with which he had left. I said that I thought that it might have had something to do with me.

"Yes," Raoul said, "he asked me whether you belonged to me. I told him you belonged to yourself."

That night, very late, after everyone had gone and he had locked the doors and cleared the tables, Raoul and I made love in the bar. We didn't bother to undress. He pushed my skirt up round my waist and pulled my pants down. It was frenzied, extreme and uncomfortable, more pain than pleasure, more fuel for fantasy than the stuff of easy gratification. The lights were dim and the music was loud. All evening we had been smoking dope and drinking rum, and though I didn't feel at all drunk, I did feel profoundly involved – I remember the sharp edge of the bench digging into my calves, and that I kept shifting slightly to try to get more comfortable, which did not in any way interfere with the intense excitement of the moment. I also felt curiously detached, as if my real self was floating near the ceiling and watching these two figures below; as if there were a single spotlight concentrated on the lovers – as if they/we were caught in the flash of a camera, or strobe, and as if the woman with the long red silk skirt bunched up round her waist was not really me but a stranger.

It was almost three in the morning when we came to; Raoul cooked a huge steak for himself, then ate it. Fatigue, drink, dope and sex had exhausted me, but Raoul seemed untouched – if anything he was reinvigorated by excess.

I spent the rest of that night in a state of semi-somnolence. I never seemed to properly go to sleep. Raoul had left the radio playing softly and all night songs from my past filtered into my consciousness. I was never sure whether I had really heard them or just dreamt them. It was terribly hot and despite a pine-scented candle that was supposed to deter mosquitoes, there was one buzzing somewhere. I tossed and turned, drifting in and out of sleep. Raoul lay on his back – oblivious, relaxed.

I had to get up at dawn to catch the six o'clock boat to

Pointe-à-Pitre. At five I woke Raoul. He opened his big strange eyes, said it was far too early and to wake him again when I was ready to go. Then he went back to sleep, sinking effortlessly into deep slumber. We left half an hour later and I caught the boat, with time to spare. Raoul came on board and breakfasted on black coffee and *tourments d'amour* – little coconut cakes which were a speciality of Les Saintes. I couldn't eat anything. I was not particularly sad to say goodbye to him – rather I was relieved to have survived our encounter; I was looking forward to hours and hours of sleep. Yet of all my lovers in the Caribbean, Raoul was by far the most compelling, and the way in which, even now, he enters my dreams – more often than not as a malignant presence – is a testament to the force of his personality and to the havoc he wreaked on my subconscious.

André

from
French Lessons

Alice Kaplan

Alice Kaplan was educated at Berkeley and Yale, and teaches French literature at Yale University. Her books include *Reproductions of Banality: Fascism, Literature, and French Intellectual Life*.

I met André at the first party of the year in Pau, where our junior-year-abroad group had a six-week orientation before settling down in Bordeaux. He came bounding into the room at me. He was long and wiry with shiny black hair and a devil smile on his face. He sat me down on the couch, put one hand on each of my shoulders: "Alors, ma petite américaine, tu t'appelles comment?" The room was packed with noisy foreign students. André's voice drowned them out completely. "Serre-moi," he said, taking his arms off my shoulders and holding them out toward me. I didn't know those words in French but I figured out exactly what they meant from André's body: "Serre-moi" meant 'hold me'. Ten minutes later I went with him into the nearest bedroom – I was in love with my own recklessness – and he put his shirt on a lamp for just the right amount of light. We got into bed and his shirt caught on fire. It was like that with him, sudden blazes; he was always jumping up to put out some fire or other, leaping and howling at his own antics. His main activities were mountain climbing (the Pyrenees), painting and chasing women. He was twenty-seven and he worked for a graphic arts firm, but it was impossible to think of him as an office worker.

I used to wait for him to come into the café around seven. He entered the room like a mannequin, one shoulder slightly behind the other and his legs in front of him. His smile was subtle and controlled; no teeth showed. He had a way of stopping to survey the room before coming over to my table that made me hold my breath for fear he wouldn't come. He looked down his greyhound nose at each of my girlfriends, bent his long frame forward to give the ceremonial kiss on each cheek, all around the table. I was last. I got four kisses, two on each cheek, with the same geometric precision.

I liked to watch André sitting across from me at the café, smoking his cigarette with his head tilted to one side to show off his cheek bones. He exuded an Egyptian beauty, his jet-black hair bouncing off his shoulders, his long muscles showing through his skin. There was so much energy in that body, it seemed to be in motion even when he was sitting.

He was a moralist and he had theories. He talked about his 'aesthetic folly' – his drunken outings – and about 'the bourgeois complacency' of most women (their desire for commitment and stability; his love of freedom). He thought American women talked too much, but he liked me because I was natural. Although I shouldn't wear so much black.

I kept a diary and I started taking notes on André: 'André ate a dead bee he found on the steps of a church'.

I liked to watch him. I studied André showering. He scrubbed every inch of himself with a soapy washcloth that he wrapped around his hand like an envelope. I watched him washing, I watched all his muscles under the soap, especially the ones around his chest he'd got from climbing mountains. I thought to myself, this is the way a man showers when he only gets a shower once a week. I thought of all the men I knew who showered every day, sloppily, and who had nothing to wash off.

I went to classes, part of our six-week orientation to French culture. In class I spent a lot of time with my head on the desk, nothing but André in it. I went to the language lab for phonetic testing and they said I was starting to get the regional Gascon accent in my r's, I should watch out. I had been studying André too hard.

We read André Bazin and learned the difference between Hollywood film and the French *cinéma d'auteur*, film so marked by the style of its director you can say it has an author, like a book. One day we were all bused to the Casino in Pau, to watch Alain Resnais and Marguerite Duras's *Hiroshima mon amour* on a big screen. The movie begins with lovers, a French actress and a Japanese architect. In the first frames, you see their bodies close up, their sweat mixed with shiny sprinkles that look like ash – the ash of the atomic bomb in Hiroshima. I watched their bodies and I heard their voices. The dialogue is sparse in this movie, the sentences are as simple as sentences in a first-year language text, except that they are erotic. One staccato statement after another, the pronoun 'tu' – the familiar 'you' – in every sentence. The movie taught me what 'tu' means, how intimate, how precious – "You are like a thousand women together," he says, and she: "That is because you don't know me." The sentences are so bare that they seem to mean everything – a thousand sentences packed together in a few words, every sentence an unexploded bomb. She: "You speak French well." He: "Don't I. I'm happy you've finally noticed" (laughter). After it was over, I still felt inside the bare secret world of the movie and went to sit in a park, where I wrote to André in an erotic trance. 'When I lose my words in French', I wrote, 'a radical transformation occurs. My thoughts are no longer thoughts, they are images, visions. More important – the feeling of power in not being able to communicate, the feeling of being stripped down to the most fundamental communication. I am with you, I see black and then flashes: a leg, a sex, a nose. Seen, felt, tasted. The taste of your body pursues me', I wrote. 'Like an essence.'

But André wasn't buying it. I still have the letter, stuck between the pages of my diary from that year; it has his corrections all over it. Where I wrote 'la joie de la reverse', which is made-up French for 'the joy of reversal', he crossed it out and wrote 'the joy of anti-conformism'. (One of his slogans about himself was that he was an anti-conformist.)

This should have been my first clue that what I really wanted from André was language, but in the short run all it did was make me feel more attached to him, without knowing why I was attached. I can still hear the sound he made when he read my love letter: 'T,t,t', with that lithe ticking sound French people make by putting the tips of their tongues on the roof of their mouths – a fussy, condescending sound, by way of saying, "That's *not* how one says it." What I wanted more than anything, more than André even, was to make those sounds, which were the true sounds of being French, and so even as he was insulting me and discounting my passion with a vocabulary lesson, I was listening and studying and recording his response.

He decided to take me out for a ninety-six-franc meal, for my education. *Tripes à la mode de Caen* – the stomach of some animal, and the *spécialité de la maison*. I ate it in huge bites, to show him I wasn't squeamish. Before he had too much to drink he made a speech at me, in his high moral style: "You represent the woman I would like to love if I were older and if I dominated myself. I am very happy to have known you. But I want a woman I can express myself with. You understand my words but not my language – you don't even realise how great a problem it is between us." (I wrote the whole speech down in my diary afterwards, word for word.) He tried to pronounce the difference between 'word' and 'world' in English – he thought it was funny they were so alike, and that their similarity had to do with us, with our problem. He couldn't make the 'l' sound in 'world'. He ordered schnapps for two plus a cognac, then another. He drank them all. We raced off to a disco in his Deux Chevaux. He leaped out under the strobe lights, out of my sight. I stood outside the dancing *piste* and watched him sidle up to four different women, one after another, twirling each of them around him in his own athletic interpretation of 'le rock'. His sister was at the discotheque. She advised me to grab him and start making out with him if I wanted to get home. Twice on the way home he stopped the car to weep in my lap, sobbing giant tears.

The next day I got a note that said: 'I'm sorry Alice. Hier soir j'avais trop bu. J'espère que tu ne m'en tiendras pas rigueur. Tendresse. André.' Which means: 'I drank too much last night. Don't be too hard on me.' I received this note like a haiku and pasted it in my diary.

That week I kept running over his speech in my mind. What was the difference between his words and my words, his world and my world? When I said a French word, why wasn't it the same as when he said one? What could I do to make it be the same? I had to stick it out with him, he was transmitting new words to me every day and I needed more. In fact, while Barbara and Buffy and Kacy (André dubbed us 'l'équipe' – the team) rolled their eyes about what a raw deal I was getting from this creep, I was all the more determined to be with him. He was in all my daydreams now. I wanted to crawl into his skin, live in his body, be him. The words he used to talk to me, I wanted to use back. I wanted them to be my words.

The last weekend I spent with André, we went to a sleazy hotel in Toulouse. He was on another drinking binge and we both got bitten up by bedbugs – or so I thought at the time. When I got back to the dorm my neck was swollen and my ear was all red. I was hot, and I went into a long sleep that I thought was due to exhaustion from being with André. Within forty-eight hours the

247

swelling on my neck felt like a tumour and the whole side of my face was swollen. My right eye was shut. I hid in my dorm room. When I had to go for a meal I wrapped my neck in a scarf and put a hat down over my right eye. I was almost too sick to care that André was spending the night down the hall from me with Maïté, a French woman who was one of the assistants in charge of orienting us. She was part Basque, like him, and lanky like him, only softer; she dressed in Indian prints and sheepskin vests.

The doctors didn't really know what was wrong with me, so they did tests. They tried one medicine, then another. Finally they sent me to a convent, where I got free antibiotic shots in my behind daily. I went there every day for seven days to get rid of the infection. The stark white cot where I submitted to the treatment, the nuns' quiet efficiency, had a soothing effect on me. I was cleansed by charity.

When I came out of the worst of my sickness I thought about it like this: it was the two of them against me. Two people who had the words and shared the world and were busy communicating in their authentic language, and me, all alone in my room. Maïté had something I couldn't have, her blood and her tongue and a name with accents in it. I was burning with race envy.

I spent a lot of time reading, and sitting in cafés with 'l'équipe', my team of girlfriends, and writing in my diary about André and what he meant. He wanted me to be natural, and I wanted him to make me French. When I thought back on the way the right side of me had swelled up, my neck and my ear and my eye, it was as if half of my face had been at war with that project. Half of me, at least, was allergic to André.

The day our group left for Bordeaux, André and Maïté were standing together at the bus stop and André gave me the ceremonial cheek kiss right in front of her, and whispered the possibility of a visit in my tender but healed ear. I could count on his infidelity working both ways.

*

In Bordeaux we signed up for housing with Monsieur Garcia, the administrative assistant of the University of California programme. "You can live with a family or you can have liberty," Garcia said. A family meant nice quarters and no visitors; liberty meant scruffier quarters. Everyone knew that liberty really meant liberty to have sex, and life in France without sex was inconceivable to me.

André showed up in Bordeaux two or three times that year, strictly on the run. Once he claimed he was in town doing a two-week *stage* (the French term for a mini-apprenticeship) on bug extermination with his friend Serge. He rang the doorbell in the middle of the night and leapt into my bed. His breath smelled like rotten fruit and he had one of those stubborn erections that doesn't even respond to sex. Finally he rolled away from me, muttering what I thought was "Je suis costaud" (I'm strong), falling into a dead sleep. After a few days of thinking about the phonetic possibilities ('choo-ee co stow' or 'choo-ee co stew'?), and looking through dictionaries, I decided he had actually been saying, "Je suis encore saoul" (I'm still drunk), only drunkenly: "J'suis 'co soo," as a way of explaining why he hadn't been able to come. I was still putting up with André, for his beauty and for his words.

Each room in my boarding house had a sink and bidet. Outside was the outhouse, with maggots. The other boarders were immigrant workers. Across the hall was Caméra, from the République of Guinée, who had a job in construction and was

ALICE KAPLAN

trying to study math on the side with do-it-yourself tapes. He helped me set up a *camping gaz* so I could make omelettes. He took me to the African Student Association dance where I started dancing with the biggest creep there. "Il ne vaut rien," Caméra warned me, "he's worth nothing; a first-rate hustler." The hustler danced like a wild marionette and told me what he liked: "fun, acid, women, music." I made a rendezvous with him, which I didn't keep. Caméra was angry with me, and we stopped speaking.

For weeks I didn't want to open the door of my room, for fear of seeing Caméra, his disapproving glance. I kept the door to my room closed, as though some father had grounded me. When I was out I had the energy of an escaped convict; when I was home, the righteousness of a cloistered nun. It felt familiar.

I had to go to the bathroom all the time. The more I dreaded the outhouse, the more I had to go. I planned outings to cafés, to use the bathrooms there. I knew which cafés in my part of town had clean bathrooms, with seats, and which ones had stand-up Turkish toilets. If I timed it right I could go to the best café in town, the Regent, anaesthetise myself with steamed milk, go to the bathroom, and make it home for a night of dreams. When I walked home from the café it was pitch black and sometimes a *clochard*, a bum, yelled obscenities at me. I was too lost in my thoughts to be scared.

The room became my world. Clean sheets once a week. I began to recognise the people on my street: the man with no arms, the *tabac* lady with the patchwork shawl, the old concierge and his creaking keys, and Papillon, the pharmacist around the corner. My room and I were together now; night and morning rituals established themselves with pleasantly passing weeks. The bidet was no longer exotic; I soaked my tired feet in it. I had a wool shawl that I wrapped around my nightgowned shoulders and that transported me into timelessness. I put the shawl on to read: *Le Père Goriot*, about a nineteenth-century boarding house, and *Les Liaisons dangereuses*, about a woman who controls her world through letters but is destroyed in the end. My room could exist in any century, in any French city.

The administration of the California programme arranged all kinds of outings and connections for us students. I baby-sat for a rich family who lived in a modern house. Their floor was made of polished stones. I was invited to a chateau and I wore my best dress, ready to discuss literature. I got there and my French hosts greeted me in sneakers. They were growing Silver Queen corn in their backyard, and they wanted a fourth for tennis. Of all the Americans in my group the one they liked best was the freckled jock who could hardly speak French and went everywhere on his ten-speed bike. I was waiting to be rewarded for my good French, but he got all the attention. He was having fun playing the American mascot, while I was doing all the hard work of learning their language and what I thought were their social customs. I would have been ready to pose as the Marlboro Man to get the kind of attention he got from the French. But I had veered off in the other direction; I was trying to be French. Besides, I knew his ploy wouldn't work for me: a girl can't be a Marlboro Man.

I was always watching and pretending, pretending and watching. I met a guy from Colorado. We were sitting at the French student restaurant together and I was peeling my pear so carefully, he said, he didn't know I was American. We went to the French student restaurant to meet people but no one spoke at the table, just peeled their fruit and left. This guy (his name is gone) and I made up stories instead of going to bed together (we weren't supposed to go to bed with each other: we were on our junior year abroad). In one, I would be a prostitute who specialised in American men wanting to meet French girls. The joke would be that I wouldn't be French at all. We figured out where I would have to go and what I would wear and say, and what they would say. He would be my *proxénète*, the entrepreneur, and we would make tons of money and live well.

He went off and found a French girlfriend, a real one, and the next time I saw him they were on his moped, her arms around his waist, her hair in one of those high French pony tails waving in the breeze. When he saw me he waved proudly, a little sheepish to have me see him like that in the middle of his fantasy. I waved back and laughed.

I wanted to travel on my own, be brave, but I wasn't. I was always afraid of making a *faux pas*. I took a taxi to the train station to catch a train and I opened the taxi door just as a car was racing down the street. The car smashed into the taxi door, crumpling it. It was a fancy taxi, a top-of-the-line Renault, and the driver was screaming at me about his insurance and how much my foreigner stupidity was going to cost him. He was so disgusted he wouldn't let me pay the fare. I skulked into the station, my head hung low: this was my great adventure.

*

In the seventeen years since I met André, my ear has swelled up on me from time to time, although never as dramatically as that September in Pau. When I was writing this book, it happened again. The swelling came on so quickly that I went right to the doctor, who took one look at me and said, "You have herpes simplex on your ear." He'd only seen one case of herpes on the ear in all his years of medical practice: a man who had the cold sore on his mouth kissed his wife on the ear, and she got the virus.

As I searched back in my mind, I could see the tiny little blister on André's upper lip, a neat imperfection I was determined to ignore but that turned into his legacy. My precious ear, my radar, my antenna: the locus of my whole attraction to French, and André went right for it! Maybe he bit me there, maybe he kissed me, or maybe he just whispered some of his words with his lip up against my earlobe, and the virus took.

At the time, when I thought about him and Maïté, I thought, "It's because my French isn't good enough," and "It's because she's French." When he told me I couldn't understand his language, André had picked the accusation I was most vulnerable to. Afterwards I thought, "I'll show him. I'll know all there is to know about his language. I'll know his language better than he does, someday."

After I had become a French professor, I wrote to André, and he wrote back. The nonconformist was still living at the same address, and I had moved ten times. I felt glad about that. There were a few spelling mistakes in his letter to me, the kind I'm hired to correct. But I didn't feel gleeful about his spelling, because it hadn't been spelling that I wanted from him. I wanted to breathe in French with André, I wanted to sweat French sweat. It was the rhythm and pulse of his French I wanted, the body of it, and he refused me, he told me I could never get that. I had to get it another way.

The End of the Bolster

Sara Wheeler

Sara Wheeler is a London-based travel writer whose books include *Travels in a Thin Country* and the bestselling *Terra Incognita*, which describes the seven months she spent in Antarctica.

For reasons long since dissolved in the fogs of history, in 1980 I bought a return ticket to Warsaw on LOT Airlines. I was eighteen years old, in that delicious state of limbo between the womb-like security of school in my home town and the big wide world represented by university. Nobody I knew had ever been to Poland, though at that time the only people I knew were West-country builders and their families – people like me. I was following my nose, I suppose.

It was already dark when I arrived in Warsaw, but I had the address of the government accommodation office and managed to get there on a tram. There was a scheme which arranged for visitors to stay in local people's homes. It was cheap, and I thought it would be a good way of getting to know a few Poles.

When I eventually found this accommodation office it was clear that the two enormous figures swathed in black sitting behind a vast desk found any interruption to their knitting a profound irritation. Only one of them was even prepared to talk.

A double room was all that was available, she snapped (revealing three gold teeth). I said I'd take it. It was against the rules for a single person to take a double room, she continued with a triumphant clack of her knitting needles, even if they were prepared to pay double rates. Neither, she alleged, was there one hotel room available in the entire city.

Despite the fact that I was probably the only customer to have walked into their cavernous office all week, it was plainly of no interest to this pair of gorgons that I was faced with the prospect of sleeping on a park bench. They were as implacable as the tide.

It was dark, I was in a strange city without a word of Polish,

I had nobody with whom I could share a room, and I suddenly felt young and vulnerable.

At that moment the creaky old revolving door spluttered to life. All three of us looked up. The crones muttered darkly, no doubt about the damnable inconvenience of a second customer. A tall, blond man with marble-blue eyes, an athletic figure and a scarlet rucksack sauntered into the room.

"We'll take the double," I said to the crone who could speak.

She looked at her henchwoman, and all the moral opprobrium the communist east reserved for the capitalist west flowed out from her puffy face.

The blond man put down his rucksack, and when he held out his hand to shake mine I remember that there was an elastoplast covering his thumbnail. I can't remember if he actually said, "G'day," but I knew from the first syllable that he was Australian. It turned out that he had already been on the road in the Eastern Bloc for a month, so when I explained the accommodation situation, he thought it was perfectly normal that we should share a room.

We stayed in a grim high-rise flat in the industrial suburbs, guests of a saturnine family who had been instructed not to speak to us. (In those days, Eastern Europe was still a fomenting sea of Soviet suspicion, and people who rented out rooms were rigorously vetted.) My new friend's name was Garry. Following in the footsteps of so many of his compatriots, he had taken six months out to have a look at the world. His mother was a Pole who had arrived in Western Australia as a penniless twenty-year-old refugee. She'd married Garry's father, a wood-turner from Perth, and they'd worked hard and made good. Garry, who was twenty-four, was the youngest of seven.

I felt terribly grown-up, sharing a room with a man under

some kind of traveller's code. We were both doing the mature thing – it was one of the occupational hazards of travelling hard in difficult places. We shared a double bed, but he laid a bolster down the middle to put me at ease.

Garry was a good companion, with a characteristically relaxed antipodean attitude to everything that the Polish system threw in our path. It seemed natural that we should travel together for a while. Before leaving Warsaw we paid 20 pence for opera tickets at the Teatr Wielki, and afterwards sat in bars kippered with smoke, downing tiny glasses of pungent vodka. We left the capital to wander through the echoing corridors of early baroque castles, and tore our jeans climbing to medieval palaces perched on rocky outcrops. We visited his mother's birthplace, and then travelled to the Tatra Mountains, where we swam in Lake Morskie Oko, climbed Mount Koscielec and ate spicy wild boar sausages. We discovered a whole new world – or so it seemed to us.

By the time we got to Silesia I was struggling to ignore the fact that I really liked him. I kept telling myself that I'd be betraying the whole arrangement if anything happened between us. I had somehow absorbed the idea that travelling occurs in a separate moral universe, outside the confines of normal life. I know differently now.

I had no idea how Garry felt. Then one day, at the end of our second week together, we took an overnight train to Wroclaw. Early in the morning he procured a cup of acorn coffee and brought it to me, waking me by stroking my arm. When I opened my eyes I felt a great rush of emotion, and I thought, What's happening to me? Despite all of Poland's exotic unfamiliarity, I learnt then that the most foreign country is within. I still believe that.

Neither of us could keep up the pretence. It all collapsed when we visited Chopin's birthplace, a village called Zelazowa Wola in the Mazovian heartland. A group of musicians from the Warsaw Conservatory were giving a piano recital of Chopin's music in the grounds of the estate. We emerged from the forest into a glade infused with the butterscotch light of late summer, and the strains of a Nocturne drifted over the silver beeches. We stood there in the chequered shadow of the trees, Garry rested his fingers on the nape of my neck, and that was the end of the bolster.

When it was time for me to leave Poland and return home to start university, we said goodbye outside the Gdansk shipyard. I caught a bus back to Warsaw, and watched Garry's waving figure until it melted into the cobalt blue of the Baltic Sea. I didn't feel sad. I felt as if I had embarked on a great adventure.

Garry came to stay with me in Oxford at the end of his six-month trip. He told me that when I left Poland, the colours went too; I thought that was desperately romantic. We had a lovely time in Oxford together, though I was preoccupied with the novelty of college. But we both recognised the fangs of reality gnashing at the edges of our dream world, and when Garry asked me to marry him, I said I needed more time: I just wasn't able to commit. He told me he was afraid I'd never be able to settle down, and that I had a vagrant's heart. I hated to hear that, but I could see there was no point in arguing: it was as if a fire inside him had gone cold. In the end, he saw that I was never going to be the conventional girlfriend he wanted me to be, and he told me he was going home.

As soon as he left, I decided I had got it all wrong. There were a lot of anguished telephone calls. But the months unravelled, then the years, and although we wrote a lot of letters, I think we were both trying to forget about the other. There were other boyfriends, other girlfriends. I graduated, moved to London and slogged away trying to make it as a writer.

In retrospect, Garry was right. I have never married. The funny thing is, neither has he. We still write occasionally, and last year he rang me on Christmas Day and asked me if I'd meet him in Warsaw.

But you can't go back, can you?

from
Nothing to Declare

Mary Morris

Mary Morris is the author of four novels, three collections of short stories, most recently *The Lifeguard Stories*, and two travel memoirs, *Nothing to Declare: Memoirs of a Woman Traveling Alone* and *Wall to Wall: From Beijing to Berlin by Rail*. Her fiction has been awarded the Rome Prize in Literature and grants from the Guggenheim Foundation. She teaches at Sarah Lawrence College and lives in Brooklyn, NY.

Alejandro had given me the keys to his apartment, saying I could stay with him in Mexico City when I returned. I had been looking forward to seeing him and did not feel in a hurry to return to San Miguel. When I arrived, I found his building, a nondescript apartment complex not far from the Paseo de la Reforma and the centre of things, and let myself in. I stood for the first time in this ground-floor apartment, a dark one-bedroom whose two windows looked into an enclosed, lifeless courtyard. It was a Saturday and I was a day late. There was no note for me, no sign of when Alejandro would be back. I couldn't find much to eat in the icebox, which surprised me. When Alejandro visited me in San Miguel, he always made me some soup or rice and beans.

I examined the décor. Brocade furniture covered with sheets and plastic slipcovers, rococo lamps with scenes of maidens and nymphs, one horrible painting of a large-eyed woman with her hand pressed over her mouth. A yellow television and many books, a rather extensive library, in fact, which included Hemingway and Bellow, each volume wrapped in a carefully labelled brown paper cover. The library aside, I had no idea how I would be able to spend time here, but I decided to relax until Alejandro got home.

An hour later the door opened and a strange woman with a suitcase walked in. She was extremely fat and ugly with a large black mole on her cheek and a rather mean, unfriendly face. She looked at me oddly. I could see immediately that she knew who I was but had not expected to find me, and that she was clearly displeased with my presence. I said hello as politely as I could and introduced myself. She said she was Alejandro's stepmother. Then she turned on the yellow television and plunked herself down on the sofa in front of a Mexican soap opera.

I sat down beside her. Someone named Rosario stood at an ironing board, sobbing because her father was in a fight with her brother who hated her boyfriend who'd gotten her pregnant. The boyfriend had disappeared and foul play was suspected, and Rosario, who was about to have her baby, wanted to kill herself.

After a while Alejandro arrived and he looked more than surprised to see me. "Maria," he said, "what are you doing here?"

"I cabled to say I'd be back yesterday."

Alejandro shrugged. "Well, this is Mexico." My cable had never arrived.

Alejandro quickly perceived that the situation was not a good one, and soon the stepmother began crying, yelling and packing up all of her things. She was throwing dishes into a box, grabbing her coffee pot. I went into the bedroom and tried to figure out what was going on, but she was speaking very quickly and shouting obscenities I did not understand.

After a while Alejandro came in. He explained to me that the woman he'd lived with for the past two and a half years, Angelita, was the stepmother's younger sister. He told me that Marta, the stepmother, came from a gigantic family of about a million children and that she was the ugliest and the fattest, that her rather beautiful younger sister had wanted to marry Alejandro, and that my presence in the apartment was causing a family crisis.

On weekends, Marta, who taught social studies, lived with Alejandro's father in San Luis Potosí, seven hours north of Mexico City. Three years before, Marta and Alejandro's father had left Mexico City, and Marta was still waiting for her school transfer. Her horrible life consisted of taking the bus every

Sunday to Mexico City so she could teach and returning to San Luis Potosí every Thursday afternoon. It was, he told me, no life, and he let her stay with him and sleep on his couch.

After telling me this, Alejandro digressed and spoke to me about his mother. "You see, she was very beautiful," he explained. "And after her my father did not want to have to deal with a beautiful woman." He spoke wistfully, with great sadness in his voice.

I was not prepared for the presence of an angry stepmother on a sofa in front of a yellow TV so I offered to leave, but he said no. He went back to the living room and they talked for hours, it seemed, while I read the *Popol Vuh*, the Mayan book of creation. I contemplated the interconnection between time and reality. The theory of being – pantheism. I saw spirits in animals, in inanimate things. I knew that what I needed now in my life, more than anything, was a different relation to time. I needed to put myself on Indian time. Not where hours or minutes mattered, but where I would look at the bigger picture – life in relation to destiny.

I was depressed and unhappy to be back from my journey, and I thought about how I could be somewhere on a beach in the Caribbean rather than in these dreary rooms. I heard a little more shouting, then quiet. Finally Alejandro returned to the bedroom and said that it was all right. She would accept me and I could stay in the apartment with them.

*

Alejandro loved to do housework. He liked to get down on his knees and scrub the floor. He liked the feel of the rags and the soap, the swoosh of water, the slippery floor beneath him.

After the floors he would go to market and spend the rest of the day making *chiles rellenos*, stuffing chilli peppers with ground nuts and raisins, wrapping them in a fine egg-white batter.

In that dark, dingy apartment, in that tiny, miserable kitchen, he would do the wash. He'd put a washboard in the sink and wash by hand sheets, blue jeans, underwear (including mine), all his shirts. He'd hang them up on a line that ran through a small outdoor corridor leading to the apartment. And when they were dry, he'd iron. He'd spend hours gliding the iron across cloth, and anyone could see that this man loved the feel of warm iron pressing on cloth, the disappearance of wrinkles, the look of a folded pile of clothes.

On weekends I would sit in a chair nearby, reading and watching him. I had never seen any man, let alone one from his culture, so involved in domestic duties. "Why are you doing all of this?" I would ask.

"Someone has to," he'd say.

"Did your mother teach you?"

He'd wave his hand as if the mere mention of his mother were an anathema to him. "I learned out of necessity," he said. "And now I like it."

He never really wanted my help, though I always offered it. He wanted to cook, clean, wash, scrub and iron. He knew how to make Aztec soups with avocado and squash blossoms, how to buy the freshest chicken. He spent hours cleaning shrimp. I'd say, "Should I make dinner tonight?" or "Do you want me to go to market?" And he'd reply, "No, let me take care of you." And I always did.

*

Alejandro wanted to take me to Teotihuacán, the Aztec ceremonial site on the great plain. "There are things you must know," he told me, "if you are to understand where you are." We took a bus for about an hour on that hot afternoon. As we rode, he pointed out to me the twin volcanoes, Popocatépetl and Ixtaccíhuatl. Of the latter he said, "You see, her shape is the body of a woman lying down. It is said that when her warrior died, she lay on the earth and died and that is what became of her."

Teotihuacán was the centre built to Quetzalcóatl, a legendary figure in transition from man to god. A Toltec king named Quetzalcóatl may have existed, but in Toltec mythology and throughout the Mesoamerican world, Quetzalcóatl assumed a stature like that of the Buddha – man in the process of becoming divine.

The Aztecs, who ruled this plain at the time of the conquest, worshipped two gods, each with his own set of priests. Huitzilopochtli, god of the sun and war, did battle with Quetzalcóatl, god of culture and the west. It was here at Teotihuacán, beneath the volcanic lovers, that male and female principle struggled. It was here that the plumed serpent came to represent man attempting to rise to something divine while his aggression and ego pull him down.

At the top of the Pyramid of the Sun, Alejandro pounded on his chest. "I am an Aztec," he said, "*ciento pot ciento*. One hundred per cent. Everything I am comes from here, from this place. The history of my people has been a history of conquest, of intervention, of a struggle to survive. We have been destroyed, our race defiled." He stared straight ahead as he talked. The wind blew his hair back. His sharply formed features grew more defined. His intensity rose. "You see all these tourists, all these visitors running around. Gringos mainly. No matter how hard we try, Mexico can never be Mexico. We had a revolution and got rid of the Spanish. Now we have the United States. No matter how hard we try, it will never be enough. We will always feel inferior. We will never do enough. We will never catch up. The US is always there, making us feel we are not good enough."

"Don't forget I am a *norteamericana*," I said. I had learned to make that distinction south of the border, for all Latins call themselves Americans.

"Yes, you are a *norteamericana*. I suppose I will never be good enough for you, will I?"

I wasn't sure what to think of this, and I was afraid to ask. "Don't be ridiculous," I replied. "You are already good enough for me."

He sighed. "That's not what I mean." He grew sullen and morose and after a while wanted to leave.

*

I hated the place where he lived. I could not help it, but it was a dungeon to me and I was a prisoner there. I tried to like it. I bought flowers and baskets of fruit. I tried to brighten it with small pictures purchased from street merchants. But we were living in a practically windowless apartment in a city in which I knew almost no one but Alejandro.

Every day when Alejandro went to work, I was left alone. I'd sit on the double bed, in a T-shirt and shorts, and immerse myself in death. I read everything I could about Mexico. Malcolm Lowry, D. H. Lawrence's *The Plumed Serpent*, Octavio Paz, Juan Rulfo, Mayan books on death imagery, explanations about Day of the Dead. You could not know Mexico, it seemed to me, without knowing death. Some days I'd work at the Benjamin Franklin Library or I'd go to the National Museum of Anthropology. But mainly I stayed in. I stayed in and read what I felt I needed to know.

In the evenings we went out. "It's not good for you to stay inside like this," he insisted, and he would make plans for us to have dinner with his brother, Ruben, and his wife, a truly awful woman whom Ruben had gotten pregnant. Ruben stayed with Margarita only because of their daughter, Alicia. Alicia was three and she had a burn scar that ran from her neck down her torso. Margarita had left her near the stove one day with a pot of boiling water. Only a miracle had saved her face from a terrible burn. Ruben hated Margarita with a passion equal only to that with which he loved his daughter. He adored this child and I could tell how much it pained him every time she was undressed and he could see her scar.

Some evenings we went to the club where Ruben played alto sax. He was a very attractive person and it always made me sad to see the terrible things that had befallen him. Whenever Alejandro and I spent the evening with him, we came home depressed.

Other evenings we went out with Carlos, the person Alejandro had been with the night I met him. Carlos and Alejandro, it turned out, were partners in a clothing store, and they often had business to discuss. Carlos was jovial and liked to go drinking, and sometimes all three of us would go to Ruben's club. When we did this, Alejandro would get a little drunk and dance. His friends called him Alejandro Travolta. When the music started, he couldn't sit still. He'd grab me by the hand and pull me to the floor. He knew just how to spin and guide me along. On the dance floor he knew when to clasp me to him and when to let go. Once he got going, he could dance until dawn.

*

One night I went to a public phone and called a woman I'd met in a gallery. We had spoken briefly and she'd suggested I give her a call sometime. I phoned Mrs Delano, and we agreed to meet at a café where there was a small exhibit of her paintings. Then she would take us to her house for dinner. I asked if I could bring Alejandro along and she said, "By all means." But when we met at the café, it became clear to me within moments that she was uncomfortable.

We ordered tea and tried to admire her paintings which hung on the wall of the café. Mrs Delano, who had survived the concentration camps in Germany, was a painter of fairly poor paintings depicting Jewish life throughout the ages. I found them without imagination or interest to me, though it was clear that Mrs Delano thought of herself as the female Chagall.

As she showed us her work, it seemed she could not look Alejandro in the eye. Indeed she acted as if he were not there at all. She also kept running back and forth to the telephone. When we sat down to our tea, she began to tell us how her cook had suddenly taken ill and we could not go to her home for dinner. Instead she said she'd take us nearby for a sandwich.

Her switch from hospitality to detachment was startling and finally I asked her, "Is anything wrong? I mean, is something bothering you?" She paused and then told us what was on her mind. She told Alejandro that he should leave me, that he had to think about what my parents would say. I told her that Alejandro and I were friends and that my mother would be pleased for me to have friends of different cultures.

Later when I went into the bathroom, Mrs Delano followed me. She said, "You are making a mistake. I have friends who are Mexicans as well, but they are fair, not dark." Fair, she told me, like us. Alejandro, she said, was of a very humble background.

I told her I knew that. It was, in part, what I liked about him.

But she went on. "I was going to have you both to dinner but my father would have hit the ceiling if I'd brought a pure Mexican home. He would not have allowed it." I could see I had miscalculated this woman and I was more than willing to leave, but Mrs Delano had other things to say about Mexicans. She told me that all the beggars in the city were really gypsies and thieves who didn't work because they were lazy. She said there was plenty of work to be had, but Mexicans wanted to do nothing all day. It was important to distinguish the different kinds of Mexicans, she said. "The ones of European origin, they are a different breed."

Later when she drove us back to the Zona Rosa, she wore her gloves. "I keep my gloves on," she said, "so that no one can steal the rings off my fingers when I stop at stoplights."

When we got back to the apartment, Alejandro was furious. "So," he said, "is this what your race is like?" referring to my Jewish background.

"You sound as racist as she does."

"What else did she say to you?" he asked me. "What did she say when she followed you into the bathroom?"

"She's a stupid person," I said, "forget it." But he wouldn't relent so finally I told him. "Look," I said, "I don't feel the way she does. I wouldn't be here if I did, so let's drop it."

He left the apartment in a huff and brought back a six-pack of beer. He sat down in front of the yellow television, something I'd never seen him do. After a while he said, "Is that why you won't marry me, Maria, because I'm dark?"

"Marry you? Alejandro, I really care for you, but marriage has never been an issue . . ."

"For you maybe, but what about for me?" He spent the rest

of the night sulking. "What am I supposed to do when you're gone?" he asked. When he went to get his fifth beer, I tried to take it out of his hand, but he walked away. "I don't want to hurt you," I called. He shook his head. He said it was already too late.

Words are Deeds

Paul Theroux

Paul Theroux was born in Medford, Massachusetts, in 1941. He published his first novel, *Waldo*, in 1967, and his subsequent novels include *The Black House*, *The Family Arsenal*, *Picture Palace*, *The Mosquito Coast*, *O-Zone*, *Chicago Loop*, *Millroy the Magician* and *My Other Life*. His latest novel, *Kowloon Tong*, is set in Hong Kong at the time of the handover. Paul Theroux's numerous travel books include *The Great Railway Bazaar*, *The Old Patagonian Express*, *Riding the Iron Rooster*, *The Happy Isles of Oceania* and *The Pillars of Hercules*.

On entering the restaurant in Corte, Professor Sheldrick saw the woman standing near the bar. He decided then that he would take her away with him, perhaps marry her. When she offered him a menu and he realised she was a waitress he was more certain she would accompany him that very day to the hotel, where he had a reservation, on the coast at Ile-Rousse. Not even the suspicion that it was her husband behind the counter – he had a drooping black moustache and was older than she – deterred him as he planned his moves. The man looked like a brute, in any case; and Sheldrick was prepared to offer that woman everything he had.

His wife had left him in Marseilles. She said she wanted to live her own life. She was almost forty and she explained that if she waited any longer no man would look twice at her. She refused to argue or be drawn; her mind was made up. It was Sheldrick who did all the imploring, but it did no good.

He said, "What did I do?"

"It's what you said."

Words are deeds: he knew that was what she meant. And not one but an accumulation of them over a dozen years. The marriage, he knew, had been ruined long before. He was content to live in those ruins and he had believed she needed him. But there in Marseilles she declared she was leaving him. The words she said with such simple directness weakened him; he ached as if in speaking to him that way she had trampled him. He agreed to let her have the house and a certain amount of money every month.

He said, "I'll suffer."

"You deserve to suffer."

Her manner was girlish and hopeful, his almost elderly. She went home; but when it was time for him to return home he could see no point to it, nor any reason to work. He was a professor of French literature at a college in Connecticut: the semester was starting. But from the day his wife left him, Sheldrick answered no letters and made no plans and did not think about the future. What was the point? He did nothing, because nothing mattered. He had set out on this trip feeling lucky, if a bit burdened by his wife. Now the summer was over, his wife had left him, and he began to believe that she had taken the world with her.

He no longer recognised the importance of anything he had ever done before, but his feeling of failure was so complete he felt he did not exist except as a polite and harmless creature who, all his defenses removed, faced extinction. His wife had pushed their boulder aside and left him exposed, like a soft blind worm.

In this mood, one of uselessness, he felt entirely without obligation. The world was illusion – he had invented a marriage and an existence, and it had all vanished. He was a victim twitching in air, with a small voice. What he had mistaken for concreteness was vapour. Only lovers had faith. But he didn't want his wife back; he wanted nothing.

His surprise was that he could enter a strange restaurant in a remote Corsican town and see a woman and want to marry her. He wondered if defeat had made him bold. This island, the first landscape he had seen as a newly single man, had a wild shipwrecked look to it that suited his recklessness. He would ask that woman to leave with him.

He was bewitched by her peculiar beauty, which was the beauty of certain trees he had been admiring all afternoon in the drive from the stinks of Cateraggio. She was slim, like those trees, and unlike any woman he had seen on this island. He knew then that he would not leave Corte without her. She was the embodiment of everything he loved in Corsica. The idea that he would take her with him was definite. There was no doubt in his mind; it was rash and necessary. And while he found a seat and ordered a drink and then chose at random from the menu, he had already decided on his course of action. It only remained for him to begin.

His French was fluent. Indeed, he affected a slight French accent, a stutter in his throat and the trace of a lisp, when he spoke English. But language was the least of it. She had small shoulders and almost no breasts, and slender legs, and her hair was cut short. He spoke to her about the food, but only to detain her, so he could be near her. She smelled of lilies. She brought the wine; his meal; the dessert – fruit; coffee, which her husband – almost certainly her husband – made on the machine. And each time, he said something more, trying to grow intimate, to make her see him. He had no clear plan. He would not leave the town without her. He was due in Ile-Rousse that night. She wore a finely spun sweater. She was not dressed for a restaurant: she was no waitress. Her husband owned the place – he forced her to help him run it. Sheldrick guessed at these things and by degrees he began to understand that though he had only happened upon her, she was waiting for him.

She approached him with the bill folded on a saucer. He invited her to look at it, and when she bent close to him, peering at the bill, he said, "Please – come with me."

He feared she might be startled: for seconds he knew he had said something dangerous. But she was looking at the bill. Was this pretence? Was she stalling?

He said, "I have a car."

She was expressionless. She touched the bill with a sharp red claw.

Trying to control his voice, Sheldrick said, "I love you and I want you to come with me."

She faced him, turning her green eyes on him, and he knew she was scrutinising him, wondering if he were crazy. He smiled helplessly, and her gaze seemed to soften, a pale glitter pricking the green.

His hands trembled as he placed his money on the saucer.

She said, "I will bring you your change."

Then she was gone. Sheldrick forced himself to stare at the tablecloth, so as not to betray his passion to the man he supposed was her husband.

She did not return immediately. Was she telling her husband what he had said? He could hardly blame her. What he had asked her in a pleading whisper was so insane an impulse that he knew he must have frightened her. And yet he did not regret it. He knew he had had to say it or he would not have forgiven himself and would have suffered for the rest of his life. After five minutes he assumed she had gone to the police; he imagined that now many people knew the mad request he had made to this woman.

In the same stately way that she had approached before, she crossed the restaurant with the saucer, and with some formality, bowing slightly as she did so, placed it before him. She went away, back to the bar where he had first seen her.

There was nothing more. She had not replied; she had not said a word. So, without a word, there was no blame; and it had all passed, like a spell of fever. Now it could remain a secret. She had been kind enough to let him go without making a jackass of himself.

He plucked at his change, keenly aware of the charade he was performing in leaving her a tip. But gathering the coins, he saw the folded bill at the bottom of the saucer, and the sentence written on it. The scribbled words made him breathless and stupid, the fresh ink made him flush like an illiterate. He laboured to read it, but it was simple. It said: *I will be at the statue of Paoli after we close.*

He put the bill into his pocket and left her ten francs, and not looking at her again he hurried out of the restaurant. He walked, turning corners, on rising streets that became steps, and climbed a stone staircase on the ramparts that towered over Corte. Alone here, he read the sentence again and was joyful on these ruined battlements and thrilled by the wind in the flag above him. Beneath him in the rocky valleys and on hillsides were the trees he had come to love.

He gave her an hour. At five, in brilliant twilight, he found his car, which was parked near the restaurant. The steel shutters of the restaurant were across the windows and padlocked. It was Sunday; the cobblestone streets of this hilltop town were deserted, and he could imagine that he was the only person alive in Corte. Not wishing to be conspicuous, he decided that it was better to drive slowly through the Place Paoli than to walk.

He found it easily, an irregular plaza of sloping cobbles, and rounding the statue he saw her, wearing a short jacket, carrying a handbag, her white face fixed on him. He stopped. Before he could speak she was beside him in the car.

"Quickly," she said. "Don't stop."

Her decisiveness stunned him, his feet and hands were numb, he was slow.

"Do you hear me?" she said. "Drive – drive!"

He remembered how to drive, and skidded out of the town, making it topple in his rear-view mirror. She looked back; she was afraid, then excited, her face shining. She looked at him with curiosity and said, "Where are we going?"

"Ile-Rousse," he said. "I have a room at the Hotel Bonaparte."

"And after that?"

"I don't know. Maybe Porto."

"Porto is disgusting."

This disconcerted him: his wife had often spoken of Porto. One of her regrets when she left him, perhaps her only regret – though she had not put it this way – was that they would not be able to visit Porto, as they had planned.

The woman said, "It is all Germans and Americans."

"I am an American."

"But the other kind."

"We're all the same."

She said, "I would like to visit America."

"I hope I never see the place again as long as I live," he said. She stared at Sheldrick but said nothing.

"You are very beautiful."

"Thank you. You are kind."

"Beautiful," he said, "like Corsica."

She said, "I hate Corsica. These people are savages."

"You're not a savage."

"I am not a Corsican," she said. "My husband is one." She glanced through the rear window. "But that is finished now."

It had all happened quickly, the courtship back in the restaurant, and she had greeted him at the statue like an old busy friend ("Do you hear me?"). This was something else, another phase; so he dared the question. "Why did you come with me?"

She said, "I wanted to. I have been planning to leave for a year. But something always goes wrong. You worried me a little. I thought you were a policeman – why do you drive so slow?"

"I'm not used to these roads."

"André – my husband – he drives like a maniac."

Sheldrick said, "I'm a university professor," and at once hated himself for saying it.

The road was tortuous. He could not imagine anyone going fast on these curves, but the woman (what was her name? when could he ask her?) repeated that her husband raced his car here. Sheldrick was aware of how the car was toiling in second gear, of his damp palms slipping on the steering wheel. He said, "If you're not Corsican, what are you?"

"I am French," she said. Then, "When André sees that I have left him, he will try to kill me. All Corsicans are like that – bloodthirsty. And jealous. He will want to kill you, too."

Sheldrick said, "Funny. I hadn't thought of that."

She said, "They all have guns. André hunts wild boar in the mountains. Those mountains. He's a wonderful shot. Those were our only happy times – hunting, in the first years."

"I hate guns," said Sheldrick.

"All Americans like guns."

"Not this American," he said. She sighed in a deliberate, almost actressy way. He was trying, but already he could see she disliked him a little – and with no reason. He had rescued her! On a straight road he would have leaned back and sped to the hotel in silence. But these hills, and the slowness of the car, made him impatient. He could think of nothing to say; and she was no help. She sat silently in her velvet jacket.

Finally, he said, "Do you have any children?"

"What do you take me for?" she said. Her shriek jarred him. "Do you think if I had children I would just abandon them like a slut in the afternoon and go off with a complete stranger? Do you?"

"I'm sorry."

"You're not sorry," she said. "You did take me for a slut."

He began again to apologise.

"Drive," she said, interrupting him. She was staring at him again. "Your suit," she said. "Surely, it is rather shabby even for a university professor?"

"I hadn't noticed," he said coldly.

She said, "I hate your tie."

Acknowledgments

Lonely Planet Publications is grateful for permission to include the following copyright material:

SEAN CONDON, 'Falling for Holden'. Copyright © 1998 by Sean Condon.

KAREN CONNELLY, from *One Room in a Castle*. Copyright © 1995 by Karen Connelly. Reprinted by permission of the author.

PETER HO DAVIES, 'Scenes from a Long Distance Relationship'. Copyright © 1998 by Peter Ho Davies.

PICO IYER, from *The Lady and the Monk*. Copyright © 1991, 1992 by Pico Iyer. Reprinted by permission of Sterling Lord Literistic, Inc, and Alfred A. Knopf Inc.

ALICE KAPLAN, 'André' from *French Lessons*. Copyright © 1993 by The University of Chicago. Reprinted by permission of The University of Chicago Press.

SARAH LLOYD, from *An Indian Attachment*. Copyright © 1984 by Sarah Lloyd. Harvill Press 1984. Paperback: Eland, 1992. Reprinted by permission of Eland.

CAROLE MASO, from *The American Woman in the Chinese Hat*. Copyright © 1994 by Carole Maso. Originally published in *Yellow Silk: Journal of Erotic Arts*. Reprinted by permission of Yellow Silk.

STANLEY STEWART, from *Frontiers of Heaven*. Copyright © 1995 by Stanley Stewart. Reprinted by permission of John Murray (Publishers) Ltd and Tessa Sayle Agency.

PAUL THEROUX, 'Words are Deeds' from *The Collected Stories* (pp. 71–76, Hamish Hamilton, 1997, originally published in *World's End*, 1980). Copyright © Paul Theroux 1978, Cape Cod Scriveners Co, 1980. Reprinted by permission of Penguin UK and Aitken & Stone Ltd.

CHRISTINA THOMPSON, 'New Cythera Again'. Copyright © 1998 by Christina Thompson.

TOM WHALEN, 'In the Restrooms of Europe'. Copyright © 1992 by Yellow Silk. Originally published in *Yellow Silk: Journal of Erotic Arts*. Reprinted by permission of Yellow Silk.

SARA WHEELER, 'The End of the Bolster'. Copyright © 1998 by Sara Wheeler.

LONELY PLANET JOURNEYS

JOURNEYS is a unique collection of travel writing – published by the company that understands travel better than anyone else.

It is a series for anyone who has ever experienced – or dreamed of – the magical moment when they encountered a strange culture or saw a place for the first time. They are tales to read while you're planning a trip, while you're on the road or while you're in an armchair, in front of a fire.

These outstanding titles explore our planet through the eyes of a diverse group of international writers. JOURNEYS books catch the spirit of a place, illuminate a culture, recount an adventure, or introduce a fascinating way of life. They always entertain, and always enrich the experience of travel.

'Lively, intelligent and varied . . . an important contribution to travel literature' – *Melbourne Age*

DRIVE THRU AMERICA

Sean Condon

If you've ever wanted to drive across the US but couldn't find the time (or afford the gas), *Drive Thru America* is perfect for you. Gasp! as Sean and his buddy David are nabbed by the Secret Service in DC. Watch in horror! as they narrowly avoid a knife fight in Texas. Be amazed! as they chat to a talking dog in New Mexico. And duck! as they meet yet another ordinary citizen who just doesn't like them.

In his search for American myths and realities – along with comfort, cable TV and good, reasonably priced coffee – Sean Condon paints a hilarious road-portrait of the USA. It's that rare combination of intellectualism and immaturity usually associated with early Mozart numbers.

See art, life and polyester collide in *Drive Thru America*. Seat belts strongly recommended.

FULL CIRCLE
A South American Journey
Luis Sepúlveda (translated by Chris Andrews)

'A journey without a fixed itinerary' in the company of Chilean writer Luis Sepúlveda. Extravagant characters and extraordinary situations are memorably evoked: gauchos organising a tournament of lies, a scheming heiress on the lookout for a husband, a pilot with a corpse on board his plane . . . Part autobiography, part travel memoir, *Full Circle* brings us the distinctive voice of one of South America's most compelling writers.

WINNER 1996 Astrolabe – Etonnants Voyageurs award for the best work of travel literature published in France.

THE GATES OF DAMASCUS
Lieve Joris (translated by Sam Garrett)

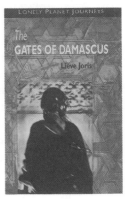

This best-selling book is a beautifully drawn portrait of day-to-day life in modern Syria. Through her intimate contact with local people, Lieve Joris draws us into the fascinating world that lies behind the gates of Damascus. Hala's husband is a political prisoner, jailed for his opposition to the Assad regime; through the author's friendship with Hala we see how Syrian politics impacts on the lives of ordinary people.

Written after the Gulf War, *The Gates of Damascus* offers a unique insight into the complexities of the Arab world.

IN RAJASTHAN
Royina Grewal

As she writes of her travels through
Rajasthan, Indian writer Royina Grewal
takes us behind the exotic facade of this
fabled destination: here is an insider's
perceptive account of India's most
colourful state. *In Rajasthan* discusses
folk music and architecture, feudal
traditions and regional cuisine . . . Most
of all, it focuses on people – from
maharajas to camel trainers, from
politicians to itinerant snake charmers –
to convey the excitement and challen-
ges of a region in transition.

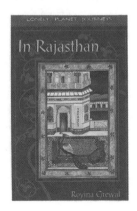

ISLANDS IN THE CLOUDS
Travels in the Highlands of New Guinea
Isabella Tree

This is the fascinating account of a journey to the remote and beautiful
Highlands of Papua New Guinea and
Irian Jaya: one of the most extraordinary and dangerous regions on the
planet. The author travels with a PNG
Highlander who introduces her to his
intriguing and complex world, which
is changing rapidly as it collides with
twentieth-century technology and the
island's developing social and political
systems. *Islands in the Clouds* is a
thoughtful, moving book, full of insights into a region that is rarely noticed
by the rest of the world.

KINGDOM OF THE FILM STARS
Journey into Jordan
Annie Caulfield

Kingdom of the Film Stars is a travel book and a love story. With honesty and humour, Annie Caulfield writes of travelling in Jordan and falling in love with a Bedouin with film-star looks.

The author offers fascinating insights into the country – from the tent life of traditional women to the hustle of downtown Amman. *Kingdom of the Film Stars* unpicks tight-woven Western myths about the Arab world, presenting cultural and political issues within the intimate framework of a compelling love story.

LOST JAPAN
Alex Kerr

Lost Japan draws on the author's personal experiences of Japan over thirty years. Alex Kerr takes his readers on a backstage tour, exploring different facets of his involvement with the country: friendships with Kabuki actors, buying and selling art, studying calligraphy, exploring rarely visited temples and shrines . . .

The Japanese edition of this book was awarded the 1994 Shincho Gakugei Literature Prize for the best work of non-fiction: the first time a foreigner has won this prestigious award.

THE OLIVE GROVE
Travels in Greece
Katherine Kizilos

Katherine Kizilos travels to fabled islands, troubled border zones and her family's village deep in the mountains. She vividly evokes breathtaking landscapes, generous people and passionate politics, capturing the complexities of a country she loves.

The Olive Grove tells of other journeys too: the life-changing journey made by the author's emigrant father; the migration of young Greeks to cities which is transforming rural life; and the tremendous impact of tourism on Greek society. A lyrical homage to Greece and its people.

THE RAINBIRD
A Central African Journey
Jan Brokken (translated by Sam Garrett)

The Rainbird is a classic travel story. Following in the footsteps of famous Europeans such as Albert Schweitzer and H.M. Stanley, Jan Brokken journeyed to Gabon in central Africa. A kaleidoscope of adventures and anecdotes, *The Rainbird* brilliantly chronicles the encounter between Africa and Europe as it was acted out on a side-street of history. It is also the compelling, immensely readable account of the author's own travels in one of the most remote and mysterious regions of Africa.

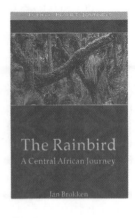

SEAN & DAVID'S LONG DRIVE

Sean Condon

Sean and David are young townies who have rarely strayed beyond city limits. One day, for no good reason, they set out to discover their homeland, and what follows is a wildly entertaining adventure that covers half of Australia. Highlights include the weekly Hair Wax Report and a Croc-Spotting with Stew adventure.

Sean Condon has written a hilarious, offbeat road book that mixes sharp insights with deadpan humour and outright lies.

SHOPPING FOR BUDDHAS

Jeff Greenwald

Shopping for Buddhas is Jeff Greenwald's story of his obsessive search for the perfect Buddha statue. In the backstreets of Kathmandu, he discovers more than he bargained for . . . and his souvenir-hunting turns into an ironic metaphor for the clash between spiritual riches and material greed. Politics, religion and serious shopping collide in this witty account of an enlightening visit to Nepal.

WINNER of the Gold Medal for the Best Travel Book, Society of American Travel Writers' Lowell Thomas Journalism Awards.

SONGS TO AN AFRICAN SUNSET
A Zimbabwean Story
Sekai Nzenza-Shand

Songs to an African Sunset braids vividly personal stories into an intimate
picture of contemporary Zimbabwe.
Returning to her family's village after
many years in the West, Sekai Nzenza-
Shand discovers a world where ancestor
worship, polygamy and witchcraft still
govern the rhythms of daily life – and
where drought, deforestation and AIDS
have wrought devastating changes. With
insight and affection, she explores a culture torn between respect for the old
ways and the irresistible pull of the new.

PLANET TALK

Lonely Planet's FREE quarterly newsletter

Every issue of PLANET TALK is packed with up-to-date travel news and advice including:

- a letter from Lonely Planet founders Tony and Maureen Wheeler
- travel diary from a Lonely Planet author – find out what it's really like out on the road
- feature article on an important and topical travel issue
- a selection of recent letters from our readers
- the latest travel news from all over the world
- details on Lonely Planet's new and forthcoming releases

To join our mailing list contact any Lonely Planet office.

LONELY PLANET PUBLICATIONS

Australia: PO Box 617, Hawthorn 3122, Victoria
tel: (03) 9819 1877 fax: (03) 9819 6459
e-mail: talk2us@lonelyplanet.com.au

USA: Embarcadero West, 155 Filbert St, Suite 251,
Oakland, CA 94607
tel: (510) 893 8555 TOLL FREE: 800 275-8555
fax: (510) 893 8563 e-mail: info@lonelyplanet.com

UK: 10a Spring Place, London NW5 3BH
tel: (0171) 428 4800 fax: (0171) 428 4828
e-mail: go@lonelyplanet.co.uk

France: 71 bis rue du Cardinal Lemoine, 75005 Paris
tel: (01) 44 32 06 20 fax: (01) 46 34 72 55
e-mail: facteur@lonelyplanet.fr

World Wide Web: Lonely Planet is now accesible via the World Wide Web. For travel information and an up-to-date catalogue, you can find us at www.lonelyplanet.com

THE LONELY PLANET STORY

Lonely Planet published its first book in 1973 in response to the numerous 'How did you do it?' questions Maureen and Tony Wheeler were asked after driving, bussing, hitching, sailing and railing their way from England to Australia.

Written at a kitchen table and hand collated, trimmed and stapled, *Across Asia on the Cheap* became an instant local bestseller, inspiring thoughts of another book.

Eighteen months in South-East Asia resulted in their second guide, *South-East Asia on a shoestring*, which they put together in a backstreet Chinese hotel in Singapore in 1975. The 'yellow bible', as it quickly became known to backpackers around the world, soon became *the* guide to the region. It has sold well over half a million copies and is now in its 9th edition, still retaining its familiar yellow cover.

Today there are over 240 titles, including travel guides, walking guides, language kits & phrasebooks, travel atlases and travel literature. The company is the largest independent travel publisher in the world. Although Lonely Planet initially specialised in guides to Asia, today there are few corners of the globe that have not been covered.

The emphasis continues to be on travel for independent travellers. Tony and Maureen still travel for several months of each year and play an active part in the writing, updating and quality control of Lonely Planet's guides.

They have been joined by over 70 authors and 170 staff at our offices in Melbourne (Australia), Oakland (USA), London (UK) and Paris (France). Travellers themselves also make a valuable contribution to the guides through the feedback we receive in thousands of letters each year and on our web site.

The people at Lonely Planet strongly believe that travellers can make a positive contribution to the countries they visit, both through their appreciation of the countries' culture, wildlife and natural features, and through the money they spend. In addition, the company makes a direct contribution to the countries and regions it covers. Since 1986 a percentage of the income from each book has been donated to ventures such as famine relief in Africa; aid projects in India; agricultural projects in Central America; Greenpeace's efforts to halt French nuclear testing in the Pacific; and Amnesty International.

'I hope we send people out with the right attitude about travel. You realise when you travel that there are so many different perspectives about the world, so we hope these books will make people more interested in what they see.'

– Tony Wheeler